C000063740

LET ME OUT

HOW TO ENJOY THE SCHOOL RUN

WRITTEN BY ANN KENRICK
ILLUSTRATED BY HENRY PAKER

LOLLYPOP PUBLISHING LTD.

Dedication

The book is dedicated to my children Rachel, Milo and Izzy.

With thanks

This book would not have been possible without the useful comments, corrections and additions suggested by professionals working in this field including Alastair Hanton, Vicky Carnegy, Richard Evans who provided the surveys, and the staff of Sustrans and Living Streets. Many thanks also to Henry Paker for his illustrations, my proof readers, Isabel Kenrick and Ruth Kitching, and to Richard Mayne who put together the index. Finally, thanks to my husband Mark Warby and our good friend Giles Davies without whose inspiration and enthusiasm the original project would never have got off the ground.

CONTENTS

APPENDICES

ABBREVIATIONS

CRB	Criminal Records Bureau
DETR	Department of Environment Transport and the Regions
DT	Design and Technology
ENCAMS	Environmental Campaigns
LIP	Local Implementation Plan
NCN	National Cycle Network
OFSTED	Office for Standards in Education
PCT	Primary Care Trust
PHSE	Personal Health and Social Education
PLASC	Pupil Level Annual School Census
QCA	Qualifications and Curriculum Authority
SMoTS	Sustainable Mode of Travel Strategy
STA	School Travel Adviser
STP	School Travel Plan
TfL	Transport for London

Author's Foreword

It is school pick-up time again - a rainy, dark December evening and as usual the congestion is appalling around the primary school gates. An irate mother leans out of the window of her massive 4x4 to hurl abuse at the driver of a battered Mini, which is trying to squeeze past her. A child darts out between two cars parked on the zig-zag lines in front of the school gate to cross the road, and there is a screech of brakes as another car just misses her - a normal afternoon in South London. Surely this is madness?

My mind goes back to my own school days in London in the 1960s, when we thought nothing of walking more than a mile from home to school, come rain or shine. We grew to know that route inside out and even now, 40 years later, if I can't get to sleep, I rewalk that daily march in my mind. I pass the old stone water trough, the church on top of the hill, the baker's shop window full of tempting chocolate krispies, and the cinema. Then the stepped wall going up the hill, which we scrambled up to walk along, the tall horse chestnut trees where we collected conkers; the artist's house with big windows, which you could peer into to see him at work. The reassuring familiarity of the journey sends me straight off to sleep.

This was no charming, bucolic stroll through the woods and fields to school, but it was endlessly interesting. Walking the same route throughout the year gave us a real sense of the changing seasons, a connection with the weather, the cloud formations, the places where puddles would collect, and the changing colours and shapes of the trees. We were given the standard road safety training at school, learning the Green Cross Code with the Tufty Club (Willie the Weasel and Tufty the Squirrel) because it was taken for granted that all the pupils would walk to school.

After primary school, I went on to secondary school in Hammersmith - too far to walk from home - and although my parents did have a battered old Hillman Imp, I can't ever remember being given a lift to or from school - even in the most appalling weather. Both my parents worked, but that was not the main reason; friends whose mothers did not work were in the same boat. My only real memories of the family car are long drives to Scotland for the summer holiday and playing a game that involved my eccentric father putting the four of us in the car with blindfolds and driving us to the other end of London. We would be deposited in two pairs in different locations and had to try to find our way home using a Red Rover bus pass. We were not even in our teens but we certainly learnt how to find our way around London pretty quickly! To get to school, we usually took the Tube or the 88 bus part of the way and walked the rest. Sometimes I cycled in on the back roads, avoiding the crossroads that have now replaced by the Shepherd's Bush roundabout. For a few months, I even walked the four mile journey there and back as training for a holiday walking Hadrian's Wall from Carlisle to Newcastle. But since then I have grown up, spent a happy few years cycling around Oxford, married and found myself living in Camberwell in south London. Once we had decided to send our children to school over the hill in Dulwich we were confronted with the Great Transport Dilemma.

Dulwich must have one of the highest concentrations of schools in London. In recent decades the private schools have grown their catchment areas so that coachloads of children are bussed in from Wandsworth and Greenwich and even from across the Thames. Parents who consider their children too young - or the coaches too unsafe - drive their children in themselves. But what concerned me when I started asking questions was the number of parents driving their children less than half a mile to and from school. Even in good weather you would see them turning up early to get a parking space near the school. And I discovered from talking to them in the playground that often they would be going straight from the school drop-off to some expensive gym to spend an hour or so on the running machine! There had to be a better way.

So, what has changed since my childhood? I guess the main thing is affluence. Whilst in the street where I grew up in London there would be just a few cars parked, now they are bumper to bumper with many parked off the street in what used to be front gardens. Some people now have not just one car, but two. And the temptation is to use them. Traffic has increased by 84% from 1980 to 2006. We all know in theory that we should be taking more exercise, but we feel that we don't have enough time to walk or cycle, even though 62% of all journeys we make are between one and two miles, and nearly 75% are under five miles[1]. Parents are concerned about road safety and 'stranger danger' Yet the safest environment for a child is one I experienced 45 years ago, where there are a lot of other people on the streets walking to work or school - rather than an empty pavement with a few brave souls scattered here and there.

---

[1] *Cycling Scotland website*

Introduction

Pick a random group of 40 year olds and ask them how they travelled to school as a child – more often than not more than 90% will say they walked. Do the same with a group of young people today and the story is completely different. Of course, especially in London, with free bus travel, fewer car owners and greater proximity to school, a large proportion of children do not come by car. However, about half of children in the UK currently don't walk to school regularly, with 41% of primary school children[2] being driven to school in cars, despite the fact that the average distance from home to primary school remains about 1.5 miles. National UK Survey Results for 2006 showed that more than 30% of children aged between five – 16 travelled to school by car. In 1969, 40% of students in the United States walked to school; in 2001, the most recent year data was collected, 13 % did[3].

This book asks why things have changed so drastically in a relatively short period of time and what each one of us can do to try to reverse the trend. Guidance is already available from local/central government and from transport organisations. This book does not aim to replace those sources, but to promote them and bring them together into a manageable, easy to understand format.

We all know how confusing it can be when you are trying to set up an initiative and work with your local council. It is equally challenging for school travel advisers to kick-start school travel projects and maintain the momentum in their boroughs.

This guide contains numerous examples of innovative practice from schools and parents throughout the UK and abroad to encourage and inspire the reader.

---

[2] *Department for Transport, National Travel Survey, 2006*

[3] *US Federal Government National Transport Survey*

Chapter One

How to get started
The story of one group of schools

FIVE TOP TIPS

• become credible by forming an action group;

• don't meet too often but give each person
ownership of a particular area;

• invite key decision makers;

• be realistic in your expectations,
set definite milestones; and

• be patient – changing travel behaviour
is a long term challenge

How to get started: The story of one group of schools

Motivation for working on school transport issues can come from the school staff, local council or from the pupils and their parents. However, experience shows that it can only be truly effective if the parents are behind the project. They are the ones with the local knowledge. They are the ones who can have the most direct impact on their children's behaviour.

If you think something needs to be done about congestion around your school, the first step is to talk to other parents at the school gates, find a few kindred spirits and get them round for a cup of tea and a chat about how you might take things forward.

Make it clear from the start that you are not anti-car. The idea is not to make the parents feel guilty or force them to change their habits overnight. We are talking only about adjusting their habits for the benefit of their children. And don't forget that many households do not own a car.

 FACT! More than 27% of households in the UK don't have access to a car [4]. In Greater London, the figure is nearer 40%.

Each school is going to be different, but in our group of local schools we decided to focus our efforts on transport TO school rather than on both journeys. Nearly every child has to be in by the same time whilst after-school clubs, sports activities etc mean their leaving times are staggered, so the congestion problem is less acute. An initial meeting with the members of the PTA was not encouraging, with some outright hostility shown by parents who perceived the project as a personal attack on their decision to drive their child to school.

Nothing daunted, our next step was clearly to persuade the headteacher. A short meeting outlining our aims achieved this, especially as we also stressed the importance of the school's role as a 'good neighbour': for example, we knew that parent patrols stopping double parking at some schools had not only improved safety for the children, but also been very popular with local residents who were fed up with congestion.

---

[4] *Department for Transport figures 2002*

FACT! *During term time, about one in five cars on the roads in towns and cities at rush hour are taking children to school.*

We then planned a kick-off meeting one evening at the school and sent home an invitation home in the children's school bags (with a cartoon of a fuming mother driving her children to school) suggesting that parents who had had enough of all this might like to join us. We said that our aim was to make travel to school a more pleasant, healthy and rewarding experience. The piece below, written by a London mother Diane MacDonald, conveys starkly the aspects of the school journey that many parents have come to dread.

DO YOU HATE THE SCHOOL RUN? - South London

Diane MacDonald explains how to relax and enjoy it

"There's been a lot of nonsense talked - mostly by men, it has to be said - about the school run. The roads get clogged, apparently. There's travel chaos at 8 and 3. What rubbish. Anyone who has ever driven a child to school will know it's not only plain sailing, but that the school run is a thing of joy, and should be cherished. Here's how it works:

Setting Off

Race for the car at 8.19 - you've barely 30 seconds before you should be jamming the key in the ignition. Launch yourself into the passenger seat, start up, wince because the car radio has been left on REALLY LOUD, and it's Phil Collins. Crunch the gears into reverse and shoot backwards into next door's Volvo. No need to panic - you won't have damaged their motor (but yours will need a respray). Pull away with the nagging feeling you've forgotten something. You have - the children. Emergency stop in the middle of the road. Drag the children out of the hall, half-dressed, and set off again.

The Journey

As is usual on these occasions, the traffic will be dreadful - but this is hardly your fault. At this point, your blood pressure will be sky high.

Your heart will be pounding and the voices in your head will be screaming, "You should have left earlier!" But like any Bad Mother worth her salt you know that voices in your head are mad and should be ignored.

Distractions

There are plenty. The bloody stereo for a start. How does RDS work? What is it? How do you find local news? How do you jump stations without jumping the lights as well? And why is Robbie Williams on at every point on the dial, no matter what time of day it is? Time to put a CD on. Only at this point do you discover something nameless and horrible where the disc usually goes. Pray to God this is Marmite. But there are other things you need to be mindful of. Homework, and why it's on the kitchen table when it should be in the car. The spelling test is this morning and you should have been practising 'where, wonder and whether' last weekend instead of drinking red wine and watching the end of 'Sex & the City'.

Yellow Boxes

Purists would have it that you can't enter those yellow boxes painted on the road at key junctions. Well, of course, you can. You might prefer to see them as bonding areas, where you can get up close and personal with fellow motorists and witness the full fury of everyone you've gridlocked. Remember, the school run is not a competition. It's a leisure activity.

Courtesy

Do you let people out at junctions? I never know whether or not it's a good thing or not. And my uncertainty is shared by others. And I'm convinced of this because the school run is full of drivers, all displaying the vehicular equivalent of a speech impediment. You start to edge forward but can't decide if that person flashing their headlights is letting you go, or fancies you, or is deriding your driving style. So you do a mechanical stammer. And both pull out at once.

Arrival

The nearest parking space will be a good 20-minute walk (or dash) from the school gates. Race down at break-neck speed, scrape your tyres along the kerb, fling the doors open and scream "COME ON!" After all, you've done this before. Grab your children by the collar and drag them to the gates. Schools helpfully place themselves in roads where it's impossible to park/stop/stroll at leisure. My son's is at the centre of a labyrinthine one-way system that gives arrivals and departures a frisson of danger that you would normally associate with Formula One.

Parking

You could negotiate a parking space nearer the school, but you will need to reverse into it. Oh no. Don't believe all that rubbish about having to parallel park next to the kerb. Fellow parents won't mind you jutting out into the main body of the road. And - despite what men tell you - it is absolutely fine to park a child's body length away from the edge.

Driveways

A perishing nuisance, despite what estate agents would have you believe. Clearly you're perfectly within your rights to punch someone if they dare to put their car even a millimetre over your driveway - and it's a public hanging if they've got a 4x4 or an ice-cream van. Especially if you're about to set out on the school run. Curiously, those same rules do not apply when it comes to your own car when you get within a mile of the school.

Hazard Lights

View these the same way Harry Potter does his Cloak of Invisibility. Not that the flashing orange lights make you invisible, but school run rules dictate that hazard lights will render you immune to traffic wardens, parking tickets, and fellow drivers. Stick your flashers on and no-one can touch you. Trust me. Now, go home and lie down. Only five hours until you can do it all again!"

Diane MacDonald is a journalist and mother of Jack, aged 7. She wrote this while sitting outside the school. If you're the Renault driver with the disabled sticker who tried to get into that space on Tuesday, she is really, really sorry.[5]

On the night, we were pleasantly surprised to welcome 60 parents. We had also invited representatives of other key groups to get them involved from the start. They included:

• School Travel Adviser from the local council;

• Representatives of local residents' groups;

---

[5] *Reproduced from the www.badmothersclub.co.uk with kind permission from Diane MacDonald*

- Governor from a local school that had already introduced some STP initiatives;

- Local councillors;

- Manager of local bike shop.

Before talking to them about our own ideas (circulating a questionnaire amongst the children, investigating liftshare databases, working on activities around Green Transport Week) we split up into groups. The smaller groups enabled parents to get things off their chests and to focus on measures that would make a difference to them personally.

The ideas that emerged from these groups included:

- Safer crossings - traffic lights/zebra crossings/more crossing patrols (lollipop people);

- Shuttle bus/mini bus around local schools;

- Re-plotting of school coach routes and/or more formalised 'buddy' system for pupils on coaches;

- Off-road or separated cycle routes for older children - split pavements for cycling/walking;

- 'Drive and Drop' schemes - several safe drop-off points from which children could walk to school;

- Pedestrian crossing at school entrances, or pedestrian access points;

- Liftshares to be promoted further with the help of postcode information;

- Cycling;

  - review of cycling within school grounds – safer areas for pedestrians and cyclists? Cycle sheds (covered desirable);

- cycle proficiency - after school cycle club?

• Public transport information to be disseminated by the school;

• Safe access from local train station into school for pupils;

• Both junior and senior schools premises to be car-free;

• Green Transport week – petrol money saved by using alternative transport to be donated to relevant charities;

• Miscellaneous – sports bags that could be carried over shoulder or with wheels;

• Involvement of pupils by use of large map where they could show where they come from (colour-coded stickers to indicate form of transport taken);

• Possibility of earlier arrival at school for some children 'early-birds';

• "Walking buses" and special 'walk to school' day;

• Preference for measures that would improve life for all, not just children (limitations of lollipop ladies).

The group started with Alleyn's School, James Allen's Girls' School and The Charter School. In the eight years since then, it has grown to include the following private and state schools: Herne Hill School; Dulwich College; DCPS; Dulwich Hamlet Junior School; Dulwich Village Church of England Infants School; DUCKS and Kingsdale Foundation School. All the above options have been explored by them. Some have been achieved and some not. Meetings have been held, clubs have been organised, cycle training has been carried out, posters have been designed and stickers have been handed out by over a thousand eager children!

The original School Travel Plans have been updated on a regular basis, giving the group access to more than £250,000 in funding to improve the physical environment to encourage walking and cycling. Nearly £50,000 has also been raised in cash or in kind to provide cycle sheds and cycle training, as well as the annual 'walk to school' weeks, which have been embedded into the schools' calendars. The map on page 12 shows the local area and the physical changes that have been made over the years to encourage walking and cycling. These include:

- Over 180 bike racks have been installed on school premises;

- Seven junctions that have been given entry treatments;

- Four new zebra crossings have been created;

- One major set of traffic lights has been installed;

- One new footpath now links a pedestrian path with the local shopping centre;

- Four walking bus routes have been used.

Appendix Eight (2008 School Travel Plan from Alleyn's School) shows that in this school travel to school in the family car has dropped by 19% since 2002 and cycling and walking have both increased (from 1% to 6% and 21% to 24% respectively). 24% fewer staff are travelling in by car.

The chart opposite shows the significant improvements at James Allen's Girls School with walking increasing by more than one-third since 2004 and car use decreasing by nearly 40% over the same period. Similar improvements have been identified in the other schools.

Lessons learnt from local campaigning

• Establish the aim;

• Establish the key objectives (make these specific, measureable, achievable, realistic and time-specific);

• Agree the target(s) – who has the power to make change happen?

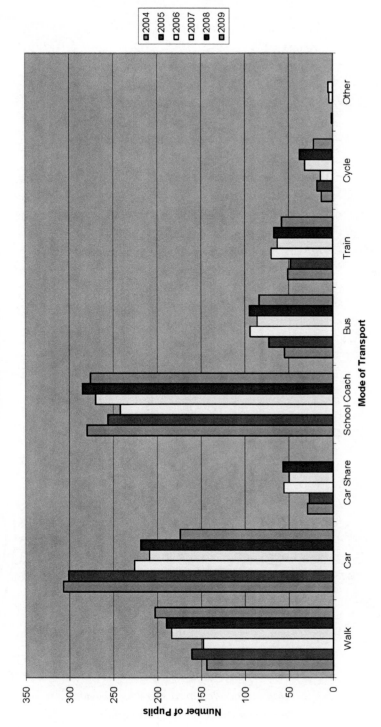

Travel Modes Summary- JAGS
Numbers of Pupils

- *What are the key messages?*

- *Traction - why is this important NOW?*

- *Who are possible allies and partners?*

- *On what evidence can you base your campaign?*

- *What will be the core activities?*

- *What resources do you have (people and money)?*

- *What are the risks? How can these be mitigated?*

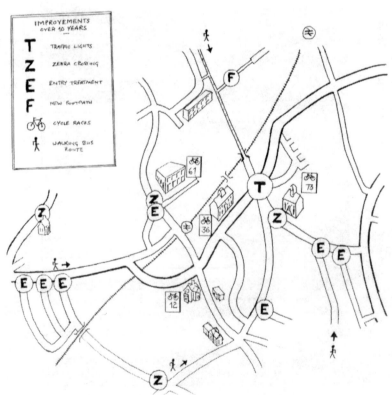

Map of Dulwich area showing physical
improvements over the last eight years,

New traffic lights at junction in East Dulwich, London

Entry Treatment in Dulwich

New zebra crossing outside The Charter School

Photos courtesy of Ann Kenrick

Chapter Two

**How to sell the concept
of the car-free journey**

FIVE TOP REASONS FOR LEAVING THE CAR AT HOME

Your child will become fit for life

You will get more quality time with your children

Your child will become more independent and confident

Your child will arrive at school alert and ready to learn

Avoid the stress of the congested school run!

How to sell the concept of the car-free journey

Changing people's habits is notoriously difficult especially when they are being asked to leave their car at home in a country where, despite global warming, the summers seem shorter and winters longer every year. From the cash-rich, time-poor executive to the single mother on benefits, from a farmer living in the south of Cornwall to a literary agent in Islington, I hear a whole range of reasons why it is not possible for their family to abandon the car and get to school by some other means.

These are the most common concerns parents have raised with me:

OBJECTION: I don't have enough time to walk with/cycle with my child to school.

RESPONSE: Driving to school wastes your time.

People often have an exaggerated sense of how long it takes to walk distances. Walking a mile in London about the time of the school run does not take much longer than going in the car. So, a lot more people could be walking without taking much time out of their day, and saving on petrol. Cycling clearly takes even less time.

Think how long it can take on a bad day to find the car keys, demist/de-ice the windscreen, sort out the arguments about who sits where, turn the car round, fill up with petrol and finally find a parking place at the school. If you walk, all you need are two sturdy legs. Biking admittedly requires pumped up tyres, but at least there shouldn't be a problem with parking when you arrive.

 "Some people don't walk because they think that riding in a car is quicker. It is but walking is about two minutes longer. In those two minutes you get some exercise."-
Morton Way School pupil, Canada

Parents and carers spend, on average, one hour a day ferrying children to and from school in the car. Two out of three car journeys made as part of the school run go straight home afterwards. Richard Evans, co-ordinator for International Walk to School, commented that when walking his child to school, he would pass parents pulling out of their driveways and yet he would arrive at school first, while the drivers were still stuck in traffic.

 FACT! *A recent survey recorded that the typical parent drives 5,000 miles each year escorting children to schools, friends' homes, parks and sporting activities.* [6]

> **OBJECTION: My child is not fit enough to walk to school.**
>
> **RESPONSE: Time to get fit then! Walking and cycling provide daily exercise patterns for your child.**

Every day, we are confronted by newspaper articles every day on the growing problem of childhood obesity, the growth of American style 'fat camps' and yet we don't always realise that one of the solutions to this problem is simply get on your bike, or start walking to school! The UK government's latest figures suggest that one in three Year Six pupils are overweight or obese and by 2050, it is estimated that some 70% of girls and 55% of boys will be overweight or obese, increasing their risk of not just diabetes, heart disease and high blood pressure – but also cancer. Do we really want our children to end up like this teenager from the US?

 "We shouldn't ever walk; I'm a high school student and this is my first year walking! Its 15 min. walking and I'm like so tired and over weary! And in the winter when it's going to be cold and temperature decreases to -7F. That's not fair at all." - Brandy aged 14, Woburn, USA.

 FACT! *A nine-year study of civil servants showed those who cycled regularly (just one hour a week!) had less than half the incidence of heart disease as colleagues.*

Walking and cycling provide the perfect opportunity to incorporate exercise

---

[6] *Children's Geographies, Children's Rights and Adults' Wrongs by Mayer Hillman, 2006*

into children's daily lives. Whilst many will do sports such as football or rounders at school, these are team games so continued involvement after leaving school is a challenge. Simply getting into the mindset that views a mile-long walk as an enjoyable opportunity rather than an exhausting trek creates massive long term health benefits for the individual and society as a whole. Physical activity promotes healthy bones in young people and prevents osteoporosis in later life. Studies of large groups of individuals born at the same time show that physical activity also protects against cognitive decline and against depression and anxiety.[7]

 FACT! Recent research at the Universities of Newcastle and Edinburgh showed that parents overestimated their children's activity considerably. They considered it to be an average of 146 minutes a day whilst in fact it was less than 30 minutes.

 "Giving our children the option to walk or cycle to school could save their lives... The upward trend of childhood obesity continues unabated... England's Chief Medical Officer recommends that children need to exercise at least one hour per day to maintain health and well-being... Approximately 30% of boys and 40% of girls do not achieve this... Cycling and walking to school are among the few ways that children can include physical activity as an integral part of their lives."- Dr Adrian Davis, Sustrans Health Policy Adviser.

OBJECTION: My child is too tired to walk to school in the mornings.

RESPONSE: Yes, they do often seem exhausted but exercise can boost your child's brain first thing in the morning.

The interesting reality that has emerged from teachers about children who do

---

[7] *Mental Capital and Wellbeing report, Foresight 2009*

walk to school is that, in fact, the exercise energises them and makes them much more alert and ready to take in their lessons. Furthermore, a recent research project not only linked walking to school with improved physical fitness, but also proved that children who walk go on to show greater activity throughout the school day.[8]

Hammersmith and Fulham Council has discovered that walking buses can help significantly with the truancy issue and with improving the pupils' punctuality. Funding has been provided for walking buses as pupils are more motivated to join their friends in a walking bus than getting to school on their own.

Walking or cycling gets results. Physical activity outdoors sends oxygen to the brain. Teachers in our local schools reported that pupils who had walked to school arrived feeling brighter, more alert and awake – and ready to learn. Research from the Department of Transport has shown that children who walked to school settled down to morning lessons more quickly than those who were driven in. Studies at the University of Essex showed that exercise helped 10 and 11-year-olds do better in exams.

 "It is super fun walking to school. Walking to school makes your mind refreshed."- Pupil, Morton Way School, Canada.

OBJECTION: Driving my child gives us quality time together.

RESPONSE: Better quality time with your child.

Throwing the child in the car and fuming on the congested roads is an awful way to start the day. Parents often overestimate the attention they can actually give their child because they need to concentrate on the traffic. Children, on the other hand, are often aware of the reality.

 'It's boring, all that 'what are you going to do today', and

---

[8] *Professor Roger Mackett of the Centre for Transport Studies at University College, London*

having to listen to Radio 4' [9]

A journey to school on foot is an ideal time to have a chat without distractions, to help them with their challenges at school or their problems with friends. This is an ideal opportunity to practise multiplication tables or test spellings. Sharing the walk to school with neighbours' children provides a whole new perspective on one's own children you may even realise your own are not so badly behaved after all! I have also spoken to grandparents who walk their grandchildren to school on a regular basis and treasure this opportunity to get to know them better. If parents accompany their child to school it can also give them the chance to bump into neighbours and friends en route.

"Most of us walk with friends or family. I walk with my grandma so she gets the exercise she needs, too," - pupil, Morton Way School, Canada.

OBJECTION: The weather is too bad to walk or bike to school.

RESPONSE: Expose your child to the joy of direct connection with the natural world.

If your day consists of moving from a centrally-heated house to a car into a school and back, you will miss the opportunity to keep in touch with the seasons. This may sound a little crazy and radical but it is common knowledge that children, as well as adults, are more stressed nowadays. This is particularly the case at exam times. Walking in and wandering home, especially if the route involves crossing a park or some other green space, can do wonders for their sense of well-being. A friend in the United States reminded me of this recently, telling me that her 12-year-old son had phoned her on his way home saying 'Mom, you have to look outside NOW – the sky is an amazing colour'.

FACT! *One in three children under the age of 11 years never plays outside..* [10]

---

[9] *Quote from child interviewed for Why Do Parents Drive Their Children To School? Transport Research Series, Scottish Government.*

[10] *Countryside Agency report*

Research by Walk to School campaigners demonstrated that children who walked developed greater powers of observation. When asked what they thought they would remember about their trip to school when they were older, those in cars mentioned objects they saw: "petrol station", "traffic lights" or "cows" whereas those who walked described pursuits that they could actively take part in, for example, "running over the bumps" or "meeting up with my friend Lexi."[11]

A research project carried out in Italy [12] gave a group of 8 to 11-year-olds several tasks to assess their awareness of the environment on their route to school. These included making a sketch map of the home - school itinerary, and reading a blank map of the quarter. The group was divided into three; one group, who walked on their own; a second, who walked with adults and a third that travelled by car. Unsurprisingly, the children who walked, either on their own or accompanied by adults, placed their home more correctly on the map and performed significantly better when describing the structure of the itinerary than children driven by car.

OBJECTION: We would have to walk/cycle along a busy road full of fumes.

RESPONSE: In busy traffic, your child is exposed to more fumes inside the car than outside.

In the congested, slow-moving traffic that many people experience every school day, pollution levels can be up to 18 times higher inside cars than outside. [13] Drivers and their young passengers are exposed to even higher levels of health-damaging pollutants than those experienced by cyclists and pedestrians. As Charlie Kronick, Greenpeace Transport Campaigner, writes: 'There is no safe haven from traffic pollution. Winding up the window won't help: drivers cannot simply shut themselves away from the effects of the pollution they create. The only real solution is to cut the number of cars on our roads.'

---

[11] See www.walktoschool.org.uk

[12] *Freedom of Movement and Environmental Knowlegde in Elementary School Children, Antonella Rissotto and Francesco Tonucci, Istituto di Psicologia del Consiglio Nazionale delle Ricerche*

[13] *Road Users Air Quality Report – Best Practice commissioned originally by the Environmental Transport Association in 1997*

It is often assumed incorrectly that cyclists and pedestrians are exposed to higher air-pollution levels than motor vehicle occupants because they are physically unprotected. In fact, cyclists tend to reduce their pollutant exposure by taking side streets and moving out from behind motor vehicles during traffic stoppages.

 FACT! *one in seven children suffers from asthma; less traffic is better for everyone's lungs.*

A survey was carried out by Surbjit Kaur and her colleagues at Imperial College London. Armed with particle detectors, volunteers measured their pollution exposure as they took a total of 584 trips either by taxi, car, bus, bicycle or just plain walking on and around Marylebone Road in central London over the course of three weeks in April and May of 2003. When the team compared exposure to all forms of measured air pollution - including larger particles and carbon monoxide - walking proved to be the best mode of transportation. "Walking is not just good for you from an exercise point of view but also from an exposure point of view," Kaur notes. "Sometimes people have the impression that the vehicle should provide some protection and that's not always the case." According to a recent report from the Committee on the Medical Effects of Air Pollutants air pollution hastens the deaths of between 12,000 and 24,000 vulnerable people a year and is associated with between 14,000 and 24,000 hospital admissions and readmissions. [14]

OBJECTION: My child could be abducted on the way to school.

RESPONSE: Crime on the streets is decreasing.

Shocking headlines notwithstanding, crime is actually going down on our streets. It is the irrational fear of crime that we should worry about. Of course, we must train our children in common sense, but perhaps 'Say no to strangers' is not the main message. The statistics on child abductions show conclusively that abductors are nearly always members of the child's family. The death of any child is a tragedy, but the comparative statistics are as follows:

---

[14] *Quantification of the Effects of Air Pollution on Health in the United Kingdom (British Medical Journal)*

An NSPCC internal survey of newspaper reports of children who were killed or who died in suspicious circumstances in the 12 months following Sarah Payne's killing (August 2000 - July 2001) found that of 128 reported cases, not one was of a child abducted and killed by a stranger. In the same year (2001) 938 children in cars were killed.

Exceptions make headlines because they are so rare. Alas, the thousands of deaths in cars go unreported because they are unexceptional. Your children will be much more confident, streetwise and able to deal with challenging situations on the road if they are allowed to go out on the streets either on their own or with you.

The idea behind any STP project has to be to assess the existing situation and work with parents and local residents to improve the physical environment in order to make the street a safe place to be. If more people left their cars at home and walked to school, both the roads and the pavements would become safer places.

 FACT! 596 children were killed or seriously injured as car passengers in 2006 By contrast, on average 11 children per year in England and Wales are killed at the hands of strangers. [15]

OBJECTION: There is no other child in my area for my child to walk with.

RESPONSE ONE: It can be safer for them to go on their own.

Your decision about whether or not to allow your child to travel on their own will obviously depend on their age and experience. However, do not automatically assume it is safer for them to go with a friend. There is evidence that children walking in a group are often less safe when they cross the road because they are distracted and busy chatting to each other. The problem is not the cars and the busy roads, it is their friends!

---

[15] *Coleman, K. et al (2007) Homicides, firearms offences and intimate violence 2005/2006: supplementary volume 1 to Crime in England and Wales 2005/2006 (PDF)*

*"I live one and a half miles away from my school and me
and my mate walk together on our own. It's great, we have
a natter and we are given a bit of responsibility too. We
walk past about four different schools and never got any
hassle."- Kate. aged 10, Manchester [16]*

**RESPONSE TWO: Give your child the opportunity to develop
confidence and independence.**

In the western world, improved children's living conditions are associated
with a gradual reduction in their freedom of movement. In 2007, 85 per cent
of 7 to 10-year-olds were usually accompanied to school by an adult.[17]

 *FACT! Between 1970 and 1991, the number of children
accompanied to school quadrupled.[18]*

Children who are allowed to walk or bike to school on their own develop a
better understanding of their neighbourhood and delight in the opportunity
to experiment with new routes. Choice of route can sometimes be surprising
– we have a lovely off-road route called Greendale, which runs downhill to
Dulwich from Camberwell, but my teenage son insists on cycling via the
main shopping street. It turns out he prefers to check out the shops and was
more likely to see his friends en route if he took this longer, busier route.

At the same time children who are being driven to school do not get as much
practical experience of crossing roads as they might otherwise. This can put
the child at more risk in the long term, as shown by this quote from a parent
who was reluctant to let her teenage daughter walk:

 *"She does travel by car the whole time. When she's walking
she's not really aware, I would think, she kind of stands and
she kind of, you know, jitters about before she crosses the road
because she's normally in the car."[19]- Mother in Scotland*

---

[16] *All quotes from children courtesy of CBBC Newsround unless otherwise specified*

[17] *DfT statistics 2007*

[18] *Children, Transport and the Quality of Life, Hillman et al., 1990*

[19] *Why Do Parents Drive Their Children To School? Transport Research Series, Scottish Government*

OBJECTION: I feel safer taking my child to school in the car.

RESPONSE: In the long term, driving your child may expose them to greater risk.

Research carried out [20] indicates that parents' protective attitudes are dependent on their interpretation of their role and on the mass media rather than on any real social hazards due to traffic or to the children's actual incapacity to move around their environment. Children have to learn how to deal with risk as part of their personal development.

LEARNING LESSONS THROUGH PERSONAL EXPERIENCE

My eleven-year-old son came to visit me at work by bus and, when he left, I reminded him to take the 148 bus from the end of the road and not to worry about missing his stop because it was at the end of the line. I did ask him to ring me when he got home. The journey should have taken about 30 minutes. Two hours later he rang me – he had taken the 148 but on the wrong side of the road, had gone all the way to Shepherd's Bush, had to scrounge 20p from a stranger and got the bus all the way back to Camberwell Green!! So he had learnt an important lesson and worked out on his own how to resolve the situation.

OBJECTION: The traffic is too dangerous for my child to walk.

RESPONSE: There are many dangers associated with being in the car as well.

Many parents cite safety issues as being the reason why they drive their children to school. However the reality is that sitting in congested traffic can lay your child open to experiencing high levels of pollution which calls into question whether they are 'safer' inside or out of the car. The idea behind any STP project

---

[20] Armstrong, N. (1993). *Independent mobility and children's physical development*. In M. Hillman, Ed., *Children, transport and the quality of life*, London: Policy Studies Institute, pp 35–43.

has to be to assess the existing situation and work with parents and local residents to improve the physical environment in order to make the street a safe place to be.

 FACT! Denmark used to have the worst record in the EU but child road casualties have declined by 80% over 10 years as a result of STP projects.

Personal safety: The facts

• The UK has one of the lowest annual rates of child death by accident and abuse;

• The death rate in the US is 2.74 per 100,000 from intentional injury and 1.58 in France;

• The GB death rate is 0.8 per 100,000.

Road accidents: the facts

• If in a car - 7 times more likely to be in an accident than if in the bus;

• If in a car - 21 times more likely to be in a fatal/serious accident than if in a bus;

• If in a car – twice as likely to be in an accident than if on foot.

Pollution: In slow moving traffic, pollution levels inside a car are two or three times more than those experienced by pedestrians.[21]

OBJECTION: The roads are not safe enough for my children to walk or cycle to school.

RESPONSE ONE: Walking or cycling can provide your child with a 'safer' context for long-term health.

---

[21] *http://cci.scot.nhs.uk/Publications/2002/09/15290/10428*

Concern about cycling on the roads is completely understandable. More work needs to be done before our roads are as safe as they are in Amsterdam and in other countries. If you are cycling and you hear a car horn sounding in France it is a sign of encouragement, whereas in the UK it is probably an attempt to get you off the road. Pedestrian and cycle training helps, as well as getting cycle lanes installed. Persuading the local authority to introduce 'no stopping' orders on zig zag lines outside schools can greatly improve safety. In Luton, these have been extended to all 50 schools in the town. Traffic calming measures such as sleeping policemen, built out pavements, new pedestrian crossings or a 20mph zones around a school can all help. With careful route planning you should be able to find a way along quiet streets or traffic-free cycle paths. And tell your child to get off and walk the bike at dangerous junctions.

> **RESPONSE TWO: Consider the long term risks of a sedentary lifestyle – obesity and associated health problems.**

Ultimately, a sedentary lifestyle is much more dangerous than an active lifestyle dozens of cyclists are killed each year in London, but premature deaths from heart disease are in the tens of thousands.

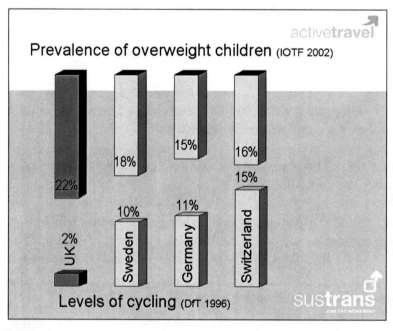

Prevalence of overweight children relative to levels of cycling. courtesy of Sustrans

Statistics from the UK National Child Measurement Programme (2006-07) indicate the prevalence of overweight/obese children at the age of four to five to be 22.9%. Further emphasizing the absolute need for primary prevention of child obesity are the disturbing predictions of the Government's scientific expert committee, the FORESIGHT team. This predicts that, by 2050, 55% of boys and 70% of girls could be overweight or obese. Research also shows that this trend is linked more to a reduction in physical activity levels than to over-eating.[22]

Not only is obesity a major risk factor for a range of chronic diseases (coronary heart disease, diabetes), but research (and common sense) links obesity with low self-confidence, low self-image and depression in children.

 FACT! *26% of girls and 24% of boys aged 11 – 15 in England now qualify as obese, almost double the rate of that in 1995.*

It is recommended that children and young people achieve a minimum of 60 minutes of at least moderately intensive physical activity each day.[23] This is defined as any activity that causes a child to breathe harder than normal and to become warmer - it includes brisk walking, swimming, dance, cycling and most sports. The school-age years are known to be crucial for shaping attitudes and behaviour. School-age children are ultimately dependent upon parents, carers and schools for their food and availability of physical activity. Research shows that a brisk one-mile walk to school that lasts about half an hour each way can burn up to 150 calories and give your child good habits for life.

Furthermore a study conducted by Mayer Hillman[24]challenged the conventional wisdom on safety and the dangers of cycling. An analysis was made in which the loss of 'life years' in cycle fatalities was compared with the gain of 'life years' in greater and healthier longevity from improved fitness by regular cycling. The life expectation of each cyclist killed in 1989 was established from road accident data and actuarial tables. The increased longevity attributable to

---

[22] *FORESIGHT (2007) Tacking Obesities: Future Choices-Project report. www.foresight.gov.uk*

[23] *NICE (2006) Obesity: the prevention, identification, assessment and management of overweight and obesity in adults and children*

[24] *Social Inventions (Journal of the Institute for Social Inventions), Vol. 25. 1992.*

those engaging in some form of exercise regime several times a week, compared with those leading relatively sedentary lives, was drawn from several surveys in the US and UK. This was then related to the numbers in the population who currently cycle regularly as revealed in the National Travel Survey.

> **FACT!** *The number of life years gained by cycling is roughly 20 times higher than the number of life years lost in cycle fatalities even in the current traffic environment which is so hostile to cyclists.*

OBJECTION: My child would have to walk past other schools and could be bullied.

RESPONSE: Get together with neighbours. Organise a walking bus or let them walk in a group.

Funny how other schools always seem more terrifying than one's own. Our local schools have implemented a scheme whereby each one finishes at a different time, to help avoid the fights that can break out at the school gates and to decrease congestion. But it's amazing what a difference it makes if you are not walking on your own. Local councils can provide training to build your child's confidence. The fact is, as Mayer Hillman comments, that 'a stimulating environment beyond the confines of the home is highly influential on a child's progress, and in the same way that resistance to germs is promoted by exposure to mild levels of infection, so too is coping with bullying, intimidation and other unwished-for events best promoted by developing defensive mechanisms based on personal experience as well as sound advice'.[25]

One thing I kept hearing from children going to school in a 'walking bus' for the first time was how much they enjoyed the chance to walk with their friends and have a good chat. My nephew, John, who walks and takes the bus to school, says it gives him time to catch up with friends before school.

---

[25] *Children's Rights and Adults Wrongs in Children's Geographies, Volume 4, No 1*

> *"Cycling and walking are good fun because you are with your mates,"- pupil at Burnholme Community College, York*

OBJECTION: It is too far to walk to school.

RESPONSE: Consider one of the many alternatives to the car that is not walking.

A maximum distance of around a mile is considered a good average for most primary school children. At secondary school, young people can walk about two miles. The journey time will inevitably get much shorter, the more you walk. Some people do live too far from their school to walk. In that case public transport, cycling, drive and drop or a liftshare could be options. However, 79% of primary school children in the UK live less than two miles from school and the average journey to school is just 1.5 miles.

> *"I like walking to school. I chat to my friends on the way and its only about 40 minutes and I keep the bus fare if I walk and it's healthy, healthy, healthy." - Eleanor aged 13, Edinburgh*

OBJECTION: What difference will it make to climate change if I leave my car at home?

RESPONSE: Show your child that you care about the environment.

Sit your children down and lecture them on the importance of environmental transport and they will be bored rigid. Give them the chance to walk or cycle instead of going in the car and they will start to understand the broader environmental consequences of their personal actions. A recent Observer magazine included a feature on the pester power of eco warriors as young as four who were nagging their parents to change their behaviour to save the planet.

As Neith Port Talbot councillor, Arwyn Woolcock, stated recently, the morning run is one of the most polluting journeys made by motorists. During Walk to School week, he commented: "Many of the environmental problems we are faced with are caused by people taking short car journeys. Cars produce more pollution on short journeys due to the engine being cold and the need to stop and start because of traffic congestion. Research suggests that worryingly, the levels of pollution in a car are at least three times higher than on the pavement at the side of the street."

Just one person who switches from driving to cycling to work or school during the week over a 10km trip each way saves about 1.3 tonnes of greenhouse gas emissions a year.[26]

OBJECTION: My child has too much to carry/my daughter can't cycle in her uniform.

RESPONSE: The school may be willing to adapt and change as part of the STP.

Schools sometimes have lockers, but pupils seem to have to drag so much back and forth with the number of activities and clubs on offer. Often it is a question of organisation – at many schools it is possible to stay to do homework at the end of school and then leave those heavy books at school. This applies to teachers as much as to pupils unless they have to dash off to pick up their own children. Uniform can pose a problem, especially at secondary school if the uniform includes a skirt which is unsuitable for cycling. However, wearing tracksuit bottoms and then changing on arrival is always a possibility.

Possible arrangements to help parents could include:

• Talk to the school about installing lockers to store equipment and outdoor clothing safely – there is money available to do this once the STP is completed;

• More and more schools are allowing girls to wear trousers as an option;

---

[26] *Verity Firth New South Wales Minister for Environment and Climate Change*

"I wish we had lockers at school!"

• Talk to the school about changing the uniform or see if they can bike in their sports tracksuit bottoms;

• Establish whether there is space somewhere for musical instruments to be left;

• If you are developing a walking bus, think about acquiring a trolley – fling all the bags in and it is much nicer walking without a bag;

• Good panniers for bikes are ideal for a lot of kit;

• Call me an appalling mother if you want, but children in my view do not need to take their games kit home every time it is worn to get it washed – once a term is often enough!

> *"I walk to school every day. It's a 35-minute walk. I enjoy walking with my friends, and we can talk. I'd love to ride my bike to school too, but my school won't get the facilities, even though loads of people want them."* - *Rosie, aged 13, Nottingham.*

OBJECTION: Cost issues – I can't afford a bike.

RESPONSE: The average British household spends £1 in every £6 on the car – more than on food or their house.

A study of school travel in Scotland[27] showed that most parents perceived the cost of car travel as very low or zero. They failed to take account of the cost of fuel, maintenance and the depreciation of the vehicle. Driving the average school run for a year costs about £400.[28] A decent secondhand bicycle can be bought for under £100. And you can forget about the cost of gym membership!

---

[27] *Why Do Parents Drive Their Children To School? Transport Research Series, Scottish Government*

[28] *SoFigure based on approved mileage rates from the Inland Revenue*

[29] *Cycling and Children and Young People, A Review, Tim Gill, National Children's Bureau*

OBJECTION: Cycling isn't cool.

RESPONSE: Start them early or encourage them to walk instead.

This objection is only really voiced by teenage girls. Younger children and teenage boys will often be extremely keen to give cycling a try, especially if they have a nice bike to show off to their friends at school. But it is a different story for girls in the UK. Go to Amsterdam and you will see teenage girls hanging around with their friends on the most individual and uniquely decorated bikes, teenage girls with boyfriends balancing splayed-legged over the handlebars and teenage girls cycling in the rain with their umbrellas up.

FASHION AND CYCLING - Westminster Council, London

This council worked with four secondary schools and six primary schools on a project involving the London School of Fashion to develop cycling accessories in an after-school club with girls. The project ran from June 2007 to April 2008 and a major catwalk event was organised to display the resulting products. The girls had a great time and loved the project, but it did not have a major impact on the numbers cycling to school. However, important lessons were learnt – in 2008 a similar project (Fashion 2 Ride) was combined with a basket of measures (cycle training, pledges to continue etc). Designers Sarah Buck and Amy Fleuriot were involved and Amy has now opened a concession at Top Shop.

What we have to remember is that the most important thing for teenage girls is talking with their friends whether on their mobiles or in person. This is not so easy on a bike, especially in a congested city. Add to that the fact that they wouldn't be seen dead in Lycra and have a horror of getting sweaty and you can understand why they present a particular challenge. But there is evidence that the climate is changing.

 FACT! *Boys on average cycle 138 miles a year and girls cycle 24 miles!* [29]

COOL GREEN CYCLISTS - The Godolphin and Latymer School, London

Charlie Blackman, a teacher and keen cyclist, reports that she has seen a change in attitudes at this girl's school. Younger girls' are much more aware of their travel habits and give fellow students a hard time if they turn up by car. About 25% of girls would like to cycle to school. The Green Team (pupils' environmental club) is being encouraged to take ownership of the travel plan process and it organises Green Weeks to help to get across the message. There are competitions between classes and points allocated to girls who don't drive in and deducted for those who come in by car. It is viewed as cool and green rather than nerdy to bike or walk. The fact that a lot of the teachers cycle and the headmistress is often seen on her bike also inspires the girls.

In 2006 4% of girls cycled to school and the target is to increase this to 6%. Bad weather and poor local infrastructure are serious obstacles but the percentage has already increased to 4.9%.

Don't even try to convert them let them walk and when they are a bit older they might, just might change their mind. Suggest they log onto www.cyclechic. co.uk, which contains masses of tips on how to avoid being another Lycra-clad anorak. This site offers advice on how to combine safety, practicality and style to achieve true cycle chic. And check out www.ananichoola.co.uk for cool clothes and products. Its aim is to produce stuff that will change the image some people may have of cyclists and make it cool.

OBJECTION: I can't possibly walk/bike with my child every day.

RESPONSE: Fine, take it in your own time….

Changing your travel habits is a bit like changing your eating habits or trying to give up smoking. If you end up driving one day because it is pouring with rain, it doesn't mean you have to give up the whole idea.

Girls cycling with style
(www.ananichoola.co.uk)

Photo courtesy of
Belinda Sinclair

Girls from The
Charter School,
London ready
to hit the road
in their outfits.

Charter pupil in
her new design.

Photos courtesy
of J.Bewley,
Sustrans

Chapter Three

What are the practical alternatives to driving all the way to school?

FIVE PRACTICAL ALTERNATIVES TO DRIVING YOUR CHILD TO SCHOOL

Walking and walking buses

Cycling

Drive and Drop

Lift share

Public transport

Pile in!

What are the practical alternatives to driving all the way to school?

These feet were made for walking!

Most people are lucky enough to be born with the most amazingly sophisticated and incredibly useful transport tools attached to their bodies - legs! It is only when people lose the use of them after an accident or illness that they come to realise just how much we all take these fantastic assets for granted. The simplest alternative to driving to school that requires no expense, extra kit or planning is to WALK.

FACT! 24% of UK citizens[30] do not walk for more than 20 minutes at a time at any point in the year. Walking with your child to school will make sure that good habits are ingrained at an early stage.

Even in the grimmest weather and the least prepossessing surroundings, as long as you are kitted up appropriately, you will be surprised at how much more pleasant it is for you and your children to make the school journey on foot rather than be cooped up and strapped into a slow-moving, metal box with you getting frazzled and the children arguing. I have already outlined the advantages – the chance to chat, to educate, to improve social skills, road safety skills and so much more.

*Two major problems were identified at **Killylea rural primary school in Armagh, Northern Ireland.** These were: serious congestion and associated pollution at the school gates, plus rising obesity levels. Teacher Margaret Kelsall worked with Sustrans and the local community to create a new track for cyclists and walkers running half a mile from the village church to the school. Two cycle sheds were built and in order to demonstrate to the community that the walk was manageable and a series of associated activities were introduced in to the school calendar:*

---

[30] *http://www.dfi.gov.uk/*

• *Whole school biking, triking and scooting to school;*

• *Dressing up and parading to school;*

• *Walking to school in wellies decorated by the children;*

• *Community picnic on the green and walk to school.*

The project started in June 2007, the track was in place by June 2008 and the results speak for themselves:

Before the project 66% of children were driven to school

After the project 13% are driven to school

Margaret commented that one little boy, Sam, who hadn't previously walked much to school said, "Mrs Kelsall, I walked to school today, I love walking, I love school!!" His whole face just lit up, he was so proud of himself. It just summed everything up! The work is continuing with competition between the classes to see which can fill up their bike shed the quickest and the school has started an environment committee which is focusing on 'Transport' as it works towards its 3rd Eco Schools flag.

Practical advice for children walking to school

• Walk in the centre of the pavement or, if there is no pavement, along the side of the road facing oncoming cars;

• If possible, cross the street at zebra crossings or traffic lights;

• Look right, look left and then right again before crossing the street;

• Never walk between two parked cars to cross the street;

• Don't run or muck around with your friends when crossing the street;

• Map out and walk a safe route with your parents;

• Use a rucksack or jacket with a reflective strip for dark evenings.

Does your school or local council provide road safety training? See if you can organise personal safety training for children and parents. Sessions could include responding to bullying, whether and where to keep your mobile phone on you, walking with friends, how to get away from trouble, opting for well-used routes, how to refuse a lift from someone you don't know, and so on.

FACT! *Walking is one of the first things a child wants to do and one of the last things an adult wants to give up*

Parents naturally worry about the safety of their children on the streets but the (perhaps counter-intuitive) fact is that a sedentary lifestyle is a far greater long-term risk to health. We need to create an environment in which our children can walk and bike safely to school. Many of the potential hazards on the way to school can be avoided or overcome. The measures described in Chapter Five (traffic calming, installing traffic lights etc) can make a big difference to children's safety and to the parent's perception of danger.

FACT! *As well as reducing your heart rate and your blood pressure, walking has been proven to reduce depression/ anxiety/tension, increase feelings of well-being, improved control of daily stresses, improve children's self-image and give them an increased sense of vigour.*

*At **Dunvant Primary School in Swansea**, pupils have found an imaginative way to improve safety around their school. With a bit of help from the police, they used speed guns to catch motorists speeding outside the entrance. The drivers were pulled over by police and interviewed by the children.*

But, of course, some parents do not have time to take the time to walk with their children and remain unhappy for them to walk on their own. The 'walking bus' may provide the answer for them.

Walking buses

What is a walking bus?

A walking bus is a way of accompanying children to school on foot. It follows a set route and a set time-table. Parents sign a consent form to join, and must usually get their children to the pick-up points in time. The 'bus' does not wait for late-comers. The ratio of adult volunteers to children varies according to the age of the children, but formal walking buses always have at least two adults.

RIPPLE EFFECT OF THE WALKING BUS ON THE FAMILY'S TRAVEL BEHAVIOUR - Lecco, Italy [31]

Each morning, about 450 students travel along 17 school piedbus (literally foot bus) routes to 10 primary schools in this lakeside city at the southern tip of Lake Como. A mix of paid staff members and parent volunteers in fluorescent yellow vests lead lines of walking students along Lecco's twisting streets to the school's gates, Pied Piper-style, stopping here and there as their flock expands. At the Carducci School, 100 children, (more than half of the students), now take walking buses. Many of them were previously driven in cars. Giulio Greppi, a nine-year-old with shaggy blond hair, said he had been driven about one-third of a mile each way until he started taking the piedibus. "I get to see my friends and we feel special because we know it's good for the environment," he said. Other parents praised the bus, saying it had helped their children master street safety and had a ripple effect within the family. "When we go for shopping you think about walking — you don't automatically use the car," said Luciano Prandoni, a computer programmer who was volunteering on his daughter's route. The city of Lecco contributes roughly £14,000 annually toward organising and providing staff members for the piedibus. The students also perform a public service of sorts: they are encouraged to hand out warnings to cars that park illegally and chastise dog owners who do not clean up.

---

[31] *New York Times, March 26 2009*

Safety and the walking bus

Every route is checked for hazards by a qualified person and he/she assesses the safe crossing points. We asked an ex policeman, who has set up walking buses all over the country, to audit our routes. Parents were asked to let us know in advance if they had specific concerns. Any changes to the routes were risk assessed. The walking bus provides an opportunity to show and explain good road behaviour to the children. Volunteers and children wear reflective vests, which the local council or local businesses may provide. These serve as an aid to the group's cohesion as well as visibility aids.

If walking buses are too bureaucratic for the setup in your school and neighbourhood, just share information on common routes informally with your neighbours.

GIVING PARENTS A CHANCE - Traffic Tamers Week, Brisbane, Australia

A group of concerned parents in Australia realised that even begin to tackle the school traffic issue, they had to see how the habit of driving children to school is formed in the first place.

They pictured a busy household on the first day of school for the first child. The school is half a mile from home, but the parent has never walked from home to the school (in fact they walk very little in their neighbourhood). The parent tries to map in their mind which way they would go if they were to walk. But they have no idea which way would be the safest way, or where the safest crossing points would be. It is much easier just to put the child in the car and drive them. It might take several weeks of walking with the child before they would feel comfortable to let the child walk by themselves. This is a significant investment of their very busy time. The child reaches the end of primary school and the parent has still not invested the time to map the best route and teach their child to walk.

To change this habit, the group decided that the household had to be given a window of opportunity, the motivation and the support to undertake the task of working out the best route and training the child

45

how to walk this route safely. This was not likely to happen with a single-day symbolic event.

In 2001 a team led by David Engwicht ran an experimental programme in Brisbane, Australia, called Traffic Tamers Week. They set children the challenge of walking to school for a whole week. (You were deemed to have walked providing you walked the last 10 minutes of the journey.) During this week they documented their adventures in a class Adventure Book. They earned Frequent Walker Points for each day they walked and the class with the most points won a pizza party. This programme 'forced' many households to invest a whole week training their children how to walk. In the adventure books there were stories of how parents gradually gave their children more freedom as the week progressed.

By the end of the week many parents felt confident enough to let their children keep walking.

Drive and Drop

Walking buses can work very well in small villages and tight-knit communities but I am sceptical about their long term viability. Parents are not always keen to sign up as volunteers, new volunteers always have to be found and the formal training required is often off-putting. In Roger Mackett's report[32] he found that lack of volunteers and excess of formality (reflective jackets, registration, Criminal Records Bureau (CRB) checks etc) were serious inhibitors. More importantly, he reported that the reduction in the number of cars on the road was insignificant so the scheme may simply give the illusion of activity and act as a diversion from other more useful initiatives.

I have found that informal Drive and Drop (or park and walk, or drive and stride) schemes hold much more appeal for parents and provide a better long-term solution.

In London, we adapted the walking bus concept to encourage parents to drive some of the way to school and then drop children off. Working with parents

---

[32] *Walking Buses in Hertfordshire; impacts and lessons, 2007*

in several areas, we identified spots about half a mile from the school where it was easy and safe to park. Car parks in local parks or outside supermarkets can provide good, safe opportunities. We drew up a rota of parent-volunteers to accompany the walking group to school one day a week. Parents would drop their children at a specified time and the group would then set off, walking to school supervised by one parent.

FREE PARKING AT NEARBY CAR PARK - Launceston County Primary School, Cornwall

In response to a request from headteacher, Carol Green, last September, Cornwall District Council provided thirty parking permits for parents at Launceston County Primary School. The permits entitle parents to half an hour's free parking at the beginning and end of the school day. This allows them to park at the council's Race Hill car park and let their children join the "walking bus" to get safely to the school. Mrs. Green explains: "Restricting the number of cars parking at the school has reduced traffic congestion and made the whole area much safer for pedestrians and for the children. More children are walking and we are now erecting a cyclepod in the playground and focusing on encouraging cycling."

Benefits for the parents include reduced time spent driving to school and less anxiety driving all the way to school and enduring the congestion. Benefits for the children include the chance to chat to their friends instead of sitting in a car listening to their parent fuming at the traffic, as well as the chance to stretch their legs and wake up their bodies before the beginning of school.

Cycling

Cycling is a brilliant alternative to the car, especially if you live just a little too far to walk to school. Everyone can remember the excitement of learning to stay upright on a bike. The bike can provide children with freedom and independence in an increasingly restrictive world. Cycling in Denmark a couple of years ago felt for me like a paradise. Helped by high taxes on cars, abundant cycle lanes and flat terrain, Denmark has developed into one of the biggest cycling nations in the world. More than two-thirds of 15-year olds cycle to school in Denmark (compared to less than two per cent in the same age group in England.) Clearly the UK has a long way to go. We need to start now and help people rediscover the joys of cycling.

 FACT! *23% of car journeys are under two miles – a distance that can be cycled in 15 minutes.*[33]

A small child obviously cannot cycle on his/her own, but there are now lots of ways to start, thanks to developments in bike technology (See page 57 for examples).

BIKE LOAN SCHEME - Camden Council, London

This council is trying out a new loan scheme where a couple of bike tent type trailers will be available for loan by parents at local nursery schools. Parents will be able to try them out to see how they could help their travel patterns.

I started taking my children to school with a seat on the back. It has the advantage being that they were in a solid, stable structure but the disadvantage was the difficulty in communicating. As soon as they were big enough, I transferred them to a mini saddle between me and the handlebars. This is only possible on a bike with a crossbar, of course, but it means you can chat as you go along. Finally, when they were too big for that, they went on the tagalong extra saddle and set of wheels behind the adult bike. This provides extra power for the main cyclist and gives the child something to do. The crucial thing is to get the balance right, with the child seat in the place with the most support and (ideally) high handlebars so that the adult can see what is going on. Guards over the rear wheel are also a good idea to protect the child's legs. This arrangement has been shown to offer a major safety advantage because cars tend to give you a wide berth!

PARENTS FOR PEDAL POWER - Richmond, London

In 2007, Jessica Anderson, an enterprising parent, fed up with the challenges of transporting her 2 and 4 -year old children without using

---

[33] *Introduction to DfT 'A Sustainable Future for Cycling, 2008*

the car, applied for a grant of £5,000 from the London Cycling Campaign to develop a bike sharing programme for transporting children to and from nursery and school. The bikes, all Dutch cargobikes, are loaned to families at the nursery. The bikes have been in constant use since the programme's inception and Jessica says: "It has completely changed the lives of parents – not only do their children love going in the bikes, but once the children are at school, we can use them for doing the weekly shop with masses of storage. I feel completely liberated and use it in preference to the car."

There are more than 23 million bikes in the UK, but unfortunately many sit in sheds getting rusty. If bikes have been sitting unused at home they may not be safe to ride. Here is a list of things to check before you let your child loose on the streets.

CHECK LIST

• Never buy a bike for your child to 'grow into'. It will be uncomfortable, dangerous and likely to put them off cycling;

• Don't buy a bike as a surprise present. The child needs to be there to try it out;

• Make sure the bike is the right size, and adjusted appropriately. The child should be able to straddle the crossbar (standing with both feet on the ground) with 2 to 5cm of clearance. The seat is at the right height if the child's pedalling leg is almost fully extended at the bottom of each stroke. The handlebars should be the same height as the seat and should allow an upright posture to enable a good range of vision;

• Check the weight of the bike – many children's bikes are simply cut down adult versions and far too heavy. Ideally it should not weigh more than 13 kilos so they can lift it up and down steps, if need be;

• Make sure the bicycle is equipped with a full set of regulation reflectors: white at the front, red on the rear wheel and at the back. For cycling after dark, a white front light and a red rear light are also required;

• Let your child have the fun of choosing a bell, but make sure it is robust and easy to operate;

• Teach your child how to lock up a bicycle correctly, i.e. to attach the front wheel and the frame to a bike rack or railing;

• Ensure your child wears appropriate clothing for the weather and season (raingear, warm or light clothing, bright clothing or reflective strips);

• Make sure your child's hand span is big enough to use the brakes easily. Ideally, get a bike with back pedal brakes that are much easier for a child. Check the brakes are in good working order with cables that are not frayed;

• Avoid overloading backpacks: install a rack or a basket on the bike instead and ask yourself if your child really needs to bring all those books home every night.

Should children be allowed to cycle on the pavement? Legally, no one is allowed to cycle on pavements, but in practice no reasonable person is going to complain about a four-year old not going on the road. However adults do need to keep on the road. Cycling on pavements is illegal and should be vigorously opposed as should cycling the wrong way down one way streets. It can terrify pedestrians, just as cars jumping red lights annoy other car drivers.

Until about the age of seven, your child can ride safely on the pavement, while you bike alongside on the road. When your child reaches the age of eight, your child can start riding with you on the street, preferably in front of you so you can see him/her. This obviously requires the child to know the route or to follow instructions shouted from behind!

There are many ways to promote cycling in your school. Get in touch with Sustrans and see if your school can participate in the Bike It project (for details, see resources in Appendix One) This ground-breaking project has seen the number of children cycling to school every day double; those cycling once a week increase from 14% to 26%; and those who never cycle to school decrease from 75% to 55%. On a smaller scale:

• Run a cycling awareness session for pupils and parents. If one of the school maintenance staff shows a personal interest, see if you can create a dedicated workshop area for maintenance;

• Install bike racks (funding is available via the STP process);

• Organise cycle training sessions preferably starting in the playground, but moving out to the roads to get pupils used to cycling in traffic. Parents can help run these;

• The appendices list many companies that will provide cycle training on the road. Funding for cycle training can also be provided via the STP. I have always found it surprising that people expect cycle training to be free, whereas they are more than happy to fork out for trampoline or gymnastics classes. One could argue that cycling is a more essential life skill!

• Organise events such as a cycle challenge (demonstrating a range of cycle skills) and/or charity rides. Stunt cyclists can even be brought in to demonstrate their acrobatic skill.

ENCOURAGING CYCLING IN RURAL AREAS - California, USA

Cycling outside towns can be scary because cars speed around winding country lanes. In the United States, people are encouraged to combine the bike with the bus, thanks to buses having cycle racks on them. This means that children living in a small village who attend school in a town nearby can bike to the local bus stop and then take their bike to school on the bus. In the UK the ban against bull bars would prohibit such innovation but alternative methods of storing bikes on buses could help a lot.

Cycling teachers as role models

Teachers who cycle in can really motivate the pupils. Some teachers have simply not considered cycling to work, but there are schemes to encourage them. Local councils can sign up for the government Bike to Work scheme and teachers can then get up to 50% off new bikes as long as they commit themselves to using the bike for 50% of their journeys to work. They then pay off the remaining cost of the bike through a monthly deduction from their pay packet. Private schools can also introduce a bike to work scheme for teachers.[34]

Practical advice for children cycling to school

• When biking on the pavement, ride slowly and watch for pedestrians; when biking on the road, stay on the left-hand side; do not ride too close to the kerb or to parked cars;

• Turning right on a busy road entails tricky manoeuvering. It is best to get off and cross with pedestrians and then mount the bike on the other side;

• Wearing a helmet is especially important for children;

• Look both ways before turning into a street from a side road;

• Always respect the traffic lights;

• Never ride between two parked cars to cross the street;

• Don't ride too fast; it's not a race;

• Map out and ride a safe route with your parent, and make sure you stick to it. Choose the quietest streets possible and bear in mind that the route a parent might take if driving to school is not always the best one for a child on a bike.

Other wheels

In recent years the kick scooter has made a real come back, especially with the

---

[34] See http://www.dft.gov.uk/pgr/sustainable/cycling/cycletoworkschemeimplementa5732

arrival of the fold up version. This is a popular form of transport, especially among primary school children. They are lightweight and portable. You can purchase scooters online from web stores or from some sport shops. Talk to the school about applying for funding with the STP to make storage for scooters, skateboards, rollerblades or roller-skates.

Nowadays catchment areas are growing and popular schools are attracting families who don't live next door. It is very important not to alienate families who really are too far away to bike or walk. Options that we found attractive included:

Lift Sharing

Even when driving seems to be the only option, car sharing with other parents can reduce the number of trips. As long as parents agree to disclose their address to other parents, all the school has to do is to analyse them by postcode and match up people. One local school asks all new parents if they wish to participate in the lift-share scheme and then produces the necessary contact details to enable parents to come to an informal arrangement.

 FACT! *In 2006, 60% of cars only had one occupant* [35]

Ask your School Travel Adviser to help with this. They should have access to all the PLASC (Pupil Level Annual School Census) data for state schools – including pupils' addresses with postcodes. This data, which could illustrate which pupils who might easily share lifts and can be imported into mapping software to produce maps that would show where the clumps were and where lift sharing might be appropriate. Incidentally, this is also a useful tool to demonstrate graphically that people live near enough to school to walk.

One can also get the data on staff addresses and conduct the same mapping exercise. Sharing lifts or demonstrating that a bike ride is a realistic option are common outcomes and the teachers then become role models for the children.

---

[35] *Figures from RAC and Department of Transport, 2006*

Coach travel

There are two options:

• Parents band together to hire a bus to take a group of children from a specific point to and from school;

• Talk to the school about introducing school buses. These work especially well if there is a cluster of schools in an area. The more children there are, the lower the cost per head.

Contact the Community Transport Association for advice on licensing, training and permits.

Yellow 'American-style' school buses

FirstGroup plc sponsored a Yellow School Bus Commission, chaired by the Rt. Hon. David Blunkett, to examine and quantify the environmental, social, educational, time and cost benefits of a nationwide network of home to school transport. It reviewed the yellow school bus system of the US and similar initiatives in the UK provided by First and other bus operators. I would argue that this is not a good option for towns and cities but may be in rural areas.

The Commission visited a number of British towns and cities to assess the benefits of existing yellow school bus initiatives. Its report was published in September 2008 and included the unsurprising but shocking finding that the number of pupils travelling to school by car had doubled in the past 20 years. The research suggested parents would be prepared to pay up to £2 per day for their child to travel on a yellow bus. Those entitled to free school meals should not be charged.

The Commission estimated that a subsidy of £154m from primary schools and between £50m and £100m from secondary schools would be needed to make the scheme viable nationally, but the benefits to the economy - which would include giving parents more time at work, could run to £460 million a year.

The Commission recommended that children living within a mile of their primary school or two miles of secondary school should be encouraged to walk or cycle. The attraction of having buses perform this door-to-door service is obvious, BUT it would be regrettable if the service were offered to children living less than two miles from school, and/or if the buses dropped children at the school gates. None of the health benefits associated with walking or cycling would be felt.

One other consideration that should be taken into account in any plans to introduce these buses to the UK is how the children arrive at the bus stops. An American teacher commented to me recently that the buses clearly ease congestion, but do not necessarily contribute to the children's fitness. He frequently sees parents in Maine drive their precious darlings often incredibly short distances to the stop and then sit in the car until the bus arrives.

Public transport

Many parents simply have no idea of what is currently available. Clearly, you are not going to suggest that a five-year-old takes a bus to school on his or her own. But groups of older pupils (years 5 and 6) relish the independence that this gives them. My nephew Guy, aged 10, has been taking the train to and from school on his own recently and has grown enormously in confidence, not least by having to cope with the vagaries of the south east London train timetable. And I am always hearing interesting stories from my children about what happened on the bus the guy whom my son sat next to who told him how he was competing in the Olympics as a shot putter; the other guy who wanted to share some fantastic music he was listening to; the time my daughter ran and ran to catch the bus and the driver actually waited until she reached the stop before pulling out!

Going on the bus and seeing the same people on a regular basis allows children to understand that there are other adults around who will look out for them in small ways (like reminding them to get off at their stop!). They may, of course, encounter some less than helpful people, but this will help them to become more 'streetwise'. In cities like London, buses are free for those in education. Failing free public transport, try to negotiate a low fare deal for pupils in co-operation with local bus companies and the council.

NEW BUS SERVICES TO DISCOURAGE CAR USE - *Admiral Lord Nelson, near Portsmouth*

When a new secondary school was built, the local council realised that transport would be an issue. Pupils lived a considerable distance from the school and there was no public transport.

A lot of work went into talking to prospective parents about their concerns before the move, about their concerns; persuading them that walking and cycling would be good for their children and reassuring them that safe crossings would be installed. Cycle parking was installed and measures introduced to reduce speeds around the school.

In order to avoid too many car journeys, the council provided first one bus, and then introduced a second. By the start of the second year, the council had to provide a third bus. The three buses operate as public services, their routes and timings determined by pupils' needs. In practice, they function like school buses. Although pupils pay a child-rate fare, this does not cover the running costs, so they are subsidised by the council's education department.

When the school opened only 18% came in a car, 31% walked, 25% cycled and 26% came on the bus. The preparatory work paid off.

Make sure that your school includes this information for parents whose children are joining the school – both in the prospectus, at any evening events to welcome new parents and in the packs that are sent out to new pupils.

At the same time you can work with the local authority and public transport operators to improve bus services. Some schools have succeeded in changing bus routes and times, as well as introducing new bus services.

Mother and children en route to school.

Photo courtesy of Chris Holt Lambeth Council

Christiania Trike.

Photo courtesy of Velorution bike shop.

Toddler Transport.

Photo courtesy of Michael Bridgeland.

Chapter Four

How to write a School Travel Plan (STP)

How to write a School Travel Plan (STP)

The prospect of trying to reduce the number of school journeys by car can be quite daunting. But do not despair, even when tempted to give up. Experience has shown that progress can be made in small incremental steps. The first task is to draw up a School Travel Plan. The work required will be rewarded with large grants and inevitable improvements.

The School Travel Plan provides a documented review of the existing set up, the preferred mode of travel for the children and the actions needed to implement this modal shift. It should be a whole-school initiative including children, staff, parents, governors and the wider community working with the local authority and other agencies.

 FACT! All UK schools must have a School Travel Plan by 2010 if they wish to take advantage of available grants

The government has recognised their value and has now set a deadline of the end of March 2010 (2009 in London – so here your school should already have one in place). Grants of up to £10,000 are automatically available on production of an STP. This standard format is nationally recognised by local councils and so any resulting requirements for infrastructure investments and financial support for cycle training etc will be easier to obtain. In most cases it is impossible to gain support without a school travel plan.

Permitted expenditure from the capital grant

- Cycle/scooter storage and wet weather changing facilities;

- New access to school and better pedestrian paths;

- Better lighting on school grounds or CCTV;

- On-site shelter for pedestrians;

- Bus turning circle on school grounds;

- Remote control system for school gates;

• Trees to 'eat' CO_2

A sample School Travel Plan can be found in the appendices but its main purposes are:

• Analyse what is currently available in the school in terms of cycle racks, provision for safe arrival and departure, parking for teachers/parents/pupils and so on;

• Establish through a survey how many children walk/cycle or come by car/bus or train and why;

• Outline what the preferred mode of travel is for the children – what they would like to do as well as what they do at the moment;

• Survey the area around the school and confirm what is already in place and what needs to be improved to encourage more children to walk or cycle safely to school;

• Set smart achievable targets and a clear action plan.

Selling the idea of a School Travel Plan to the staff and parents should not be too difficult. Parents' Teachers' Associations are constantly trying to find ways to raise money for their schools. If you explain that by completing an STP they can raise up to £10,000 for useful facilities they should be delighted. Just think how many cake sales they would need to hold to raise the same amount!

BENEFITS OF THE STP - St Augustine's Primary, Fulham, London

Mary Kelliher, Headteacher commented:

"I have got to admit that the school travel plan has made a difference, and it has actually enhanced our work on the Every Child Matters agenda. Young minds are very receptive, and the children can put a lot of pressure on their parents, when it comes to changing habits.

There is no doubt that the introduction of the cycle storage facilities has had a huge impact on the numbers bringing bikes and scooters to school. Children have really grasped the idea that as they live close to the school, driving is an unhealthy and unnecessary option!"

The STP shown in Appendix Eight is a long document and may take around a term to develop. Much of this is in small packets, e.g. running the surveys, waiting for returns, sending them to STA, waiting for data entry and results. When it comes to actually writing up the STP, two days should be enough. The key to a successful STP is delegation. Find out where the skills in your group of parents and teachers lie and allocate tasks accordingly. We found a mother who did market research and was happy not only to create a questionnaire but to analyse the hundreds of responses. This was no small task. The STA from the local council should have sufficient experience to help you with much of the STP. The school headteacher or bursar will have to sanction much of the report, but the initial draft on the existing situation and aims of the plan can be prepared by an enthusiastic teacher. Funding is available for supply cover to free teachers to prepare the STP. One of the key elements of the STP is the action plan where targets are set out, specific individuals named as responsible and monitoring processes confirmed. To do this accurately questionnaires need to establish the preferred mode of travel.

Finding out what parents and children want – the questionnaire

Getting the children on board is absolutely critical to the success of any project – pester power, we all know, is a lethal weapon, and should be harnessed. Research by Sustrans has shown that 45% of children would rather walk or cycle to school than go in the car.

If a child has a good experience walking to school (especially with friends), they will nag until you let them do this on a regular basis. The Walk Once a Week (Walk on Wednesdays) scheme has been very successful in participating primary schools.

Most parents want their children to be fit and healthy, and have no desire to waste hours sitting in traffic jams, and yet cannot see how walking or cycling to school can fit into their routine. This is why the wording of the initial questionnaire is so important. It is crucial to identify the barriers to walking and cycling at the outset.We encouraged parents to complete our questionnaire together with their child,but it was clear from the responses that this was not always happening. It is essential for a good school travel plan to demonstrate not only the existing state of affairs, but also the child's preferred mode of travel. Also effective, and more popular, was the use of mapping software in an ICT class for pupils who were already walking to school. These children not only mapped their route in, but also provided useful feedback on problem areas where it was difficult to cross the road or where a cycle track ran out. This software collated the responses from the children and made it easy to see at a glance where the bottlenecks were, which spots could benefit from zebra crossings and where, for example, a new pedestrian link over a canal or railway line would create a more direct route to school on foot or bike. Bespoke software is available but it is also possible to create this useful informationnwith Google maps (see www.communitywalk.com).

Download and adapt the questionnaires in the appendices from www. lollypoppublishing.co.uk/letmeout and modify them to suit your school. Other questionnaires for primary, secondary and special schools can also be downloaded.

> " *"I like walking to school because you get to see lots of things that you wouldn't see if you were in the car: I see squirrels and pick up conkers. I would like to cycle to school but I'm too young and there's too much traffic. If more people walked and cycled there'd be less traffic and if there's less traffic, more people would walk and cycle".*
> *- Peter aged 8, Bolton*

Setting targets

The case studies quoted in this book demonstrate the fact that different schools set different targets in different ways. Some simply aim for a reduction in the percentage of cars arriving at the school gate because their priority is to decrease congestion. Others are more concerned about the health, aspect and so they concentrate more on increasing walking and cycling. The context will clearly make a big difference, for example, the pro-cycle lobby in London is frustrated by the free school bus travel available to children which inevitably means fewer children cycling to school. But walking to and from the bus stop is often not an insignificant trek; children are is still getting exercise and eliminating a car trip, so it should be applauded. Talk to your STA about setting realistic targets to keep parents and children motivated.

Do School Travel Plans work?

I have already quoted the experience of our local schools that have made progress, but without a spectacular transformation of travel habits. Other London boroughs can also claim greater success.

Pupil survey results from annual STP reviews at 36 schools in the London Borough of Hammersmith & Fulham (with almost 10,000 pupils) show that car use is down by 33%, while almost 1,200 more pupils are now walking and cycling to school. The baseline figures are primarily from 2004. Use of public transport has also risen significantly:[36]

Changes by number and percentage of pupils travelling to school

Mode	Baseline Survey		Most Recent Survey		% Modal Shift
Car	2083	23.7%	1558	15.9%	**-32.9%**
Car Lift	222	2.5%	185	1.9%	**-25.3%**
Walk	4081	46.5%	4814	49.2%	**5.8%**
Bike	514	5.9%	974	9.9%	**69.9%**
Bus	1238	14.1%	1500	15.3%	**8.7%**
Train / Tube	641	7.3%	758	7.7%	**6.1%**
TOTAL	**8779**		**9789**		

Finally the STP must remain a live document and be updated every year to take account of new developments and new initiatives. Appendix Seven gives an example of Hands Up surveys which can be conducted informally in class. But it is also useful to monitor aspects like:

• changes in perception of children's safety in the new environment;

• changes in community cohesion;

• children's activity levels.

---

[36] November 2008 figures courtesy of Richard Evans

In many countries, including New Zealand and the UK, the concept of a national database, gathering together all the data from the surveys in schools to produce a country-wide barometer, is being explored.

Chapter Five

How to improve the physical environment

FIVE TOP IMPROVEMENTS TO THE PHYSICAL ENVIRONMENT

Traffic-calming measures

Zebra crossings

Raised entry treatments

Cycle lanes

Traffic lights

How to improve the physical environment

In Denmark, my family and I encountered streetscapes that put cyclists and walkers at the heart of town planning. In Amsterdam, I was astonished at the way car drivers were treated like second class citizens when it came to priority on the road. People in the UK tend to assume that life was ever thus in Holland and Scandinavia. Not so. In the early 1970s, Denmark had the highest rate of child road deaths in Western Europe. After Safe Routes to School schemes were introduced, child cycle and pedestrian accidents were cut by 80% in 10 years. Nowadays, at least 60% of young people cycle to school compared with just 1% here. It will be a while before the UK catches up, but we need to start now.

Bear in mind when writing the STP and deciding what is needed in your area that transport projects are expensive. You might well imagine that creating a zebra crossing should not cost more than the price of a few cans of paint. But sadly; for the crossing to be effective, a feasibility study will be needed to establish its exact position and the road surface will usually need to be raised to avoid accidents. Count on at least £50,000.

What does it all cost?

Street bike stands	£100-£150 each
On road cycle lanes	£5,000 per km
Speed cameras	£15,000
Road markings, traffic signs, parking restrictions or refuges	£15,000
Toucan crossings	£30-40,000
Pelican crossings	£35,000
Zebra crossing	£50,000
New shared use cycle paths	£65-75,000 per km

Furthermore, your council will require you to demonstrate how the proposal will produce the desired outcomes (improved safety and reduction in accidents). Unfortunately, this has often meant that approval for such measures is only given where there have been deaths or serious accidents. However there is a growing trend to look at improvements not just in isolation but in relation to general public space improvements that can have a positive impact both on child safety and, more generally, on community cohesion and economic regeneration.

What physical improvements could you make locally to make your child's journey to school safer?

Zig-zag lines

Zig-zag lines, which prohibit parking at school pick-up and drop-off times, can be painted next to the pavement outside the school for a distance of 20m. Yet not all schools have them. Check with your local authority if your school has no lines. Parents will not necessarily respect them, as our local primary school discovered. In the end, they had to introduce a rota of teachers and parents to stand next to the lines (especially in the afternoons) to 'remind' parents that they were not allowed to stop there.

> ### *STOPPING INCONSIDERATE PARKING - South West London*
>
> *One parent at a school in London was so infuriated by the persistent dangerous behaviour of other parent drivers that he teamed up with other parents to present OSCAR trophies to the worst offenders. After monitoring the drivers over several weeks to establish the rankings, they confronted the culprits and presented them with dolls that had their limbs twisted and covered in ketchup - shocking but effective! The photos on the front page of the local paper sent out a clear message to others!*

Zebra crossings

Once a mapping exercise has established the most frequently-used routes to school, you may well identify key points where traffic lights would not be appropriate but crossing was still difficult. Raised zebra crossings allow traffic to flow freely outside school journey times, but improve safety when necessary. Fiona Hanton, a mother in a rural area, campaigned some years ago to make zebra crossings outside each school mandatory. If this were taken up, it would not be necessary to lobby every council separately to do something and that would obviously make walking to school safer.

"It's difficult to see when you cross the road outside school because of all the parked cars"- pupil at Burnholme Community College, York

School Crossing Patrol (lollipop people)

These noble figures first appeared in London in 1953, but in 2000 changes in the law removed the legal requirement to provide them. Some local authorities will provide money to schools to recruit staff and will pay for insurance, training and monitoring. Unfortunately, low rates of pay as well as 'lollipop rage' (incidents with aggressive drivers) make the job unattractive. More than a third of schools in Croydon, London, are reportedly without patrols. In some cases, schools have recruited voluntary patrols among parents and teachers and used the money saved for other safety measures.

Traffic lights – pelican crossings, toucan crossings etc

One of the main reasons we set up our safe routes to school group was a very dangerous crossing in between several schools – an intersection of two main roads both carrying a lot of commuter traffic in the morning. We presented the local council with a professional travel plan which demonstrated the need for a crossing and this led to a grant from Transport for London to install the lights. Clearly such lights need to have the 'green man' option and it can take months to get the phasing right giving the children time to cross without causing undue traffic jams.

Raised entry treatments/raised crosswalks

Research has shown that raising the entrance to a road to pavement level can improve safety and confidence significantly for children, as well as older people. They can mark the transition from a major road to a residential road or can identify the beginning of 20mph zones. Additional features can include:

• build-outs and pinch-points reducing the width of the road to improve safety;

• changes in surface texture or colour to highlight the environment change to the driver;

- bollards and planting;

- tactile paving;

- signs.

The photograph on page 13 shows how a very wide road was made much safer for children to cross by such treatment. It can also significantly reduce traffic on minor roads because drivers dislike having to slow down. Rumour has it locally that several people in the affected roads have moved their bedrooms from the rear of the house to the front because it is so much quieter!

Refuges

These allow children to stop and then assess the traffic moving in just one direction. They are especially good for wide roads.

Getting a bus stop installed outside the school

Talk to the local council if the nearest bus stop is some distance from the entrance to the school. It may be possible to get a new one installed to encourage more parents to let their children take the bus.

Improved lighting

Improvements in lighting can make cycling and walking much more attractive. There is a nice pedestrian and cycle path that runs between Camberwell and Dulwich and alongside school playing fields, but at present many parents are unwilling to let their children use it especially in the winter months, because it is a bit dark and threatening.

Signposting Safe Routes to School

Drivers have no intention of going too fast, but need to be reminded that a school is in the area. Triangular road surface markings and triangular red warning signs can improve the driver's awareness of the school's location.

Bellenden School in Peckham, London

This school installed surface markings and warning signs as part of a programme to get more children walking.

Walking has increased by 22% (from 63% to 85%) since these engineering measures were introduced.

Where possible, get the children to design logos for the signs to remind drivers that they are in a school area. In Norway, they apparently have a national campaign at the beginning of each school year to remind drivers that schools about the new term and they should watch out for children. Create Safer Route Trails by marking out routes on the pavements to include the safest crossing points. Talk to the council about installing signs to the schools showing not the distances from the sign but the time required to walk the distance. This has been done to great effect in Exeter and Southampton, where attractive signs show pedestrians how long it should take to walk to the shopping or leisure centre.

SHOWING CHILDREN THE BEST WAY - Beech Hill School, Luton

Walking was the predominant mode of transport at this school but transport planners were keen to get systems in place to prepare for greater car ownership. A graphic designer worked with pupils to produce a logo that could be used to mark safe routes. They came up with a dinosaur called Trax. Different coloured dinosaur footprints marked on the pavements indicate the various routes to the school, The dinosaur logo is used on all Safety around Schools publicity to help brand the initiative across all local schools.

Traffic calming measures

Slowing traffic down by introducing sleeping policemen and/or narrowing the road at critical points can make the roads safer to cross and to cycle on. Local reviews of speed cushions demonstrate that they are far less effective in reducing the driver's speed than full width speed bumps. Flashing signs can remind drivers that they are in a school area.

REMINDING DRIVERS TO KEEP THEIR SPEED DOWN - St Mary's Primary School, Derrytrasna Northern Ireland

The principal, Joan Aldridge, had concerns about the pupils' safety around the school. In this rural area there were problems both with speeding cars and congestion at the school gate. Working with Sustrans and following the preparation of a School Travel Plan in 2007, it was decided that the best solution was flashing lights to remind drivers to keep their speed down. These solar-powered panels were installed and programmed to operate at school drop-off and pick-up times. Ms Aldridge spoke proudly of the difference the project had made to the school: "Friday is walk to school day and it is set in stone. Even in the bad January weather pupils and teachers all walked in. Some come on their own; others join up at two meeting points and come in a group. The pupils are very enthusiastic, the parents are much happier to let their children walk on their own and the knock-on effect has been considerable. I didn't realise that the biggest change in our school would be in our attitudes. Teachers now take the classes out walking as part of the lessons which they would never have done before."

Before the initiative, 81.8% of pupils were being driven to school. After the project this dropped to 51.5%.

20mph zones around schools

Slowing traffic down around schools makes a big difference to the safety of children walking or biking in to school. In towns where it is hard to install new cycle lanes, bringing the speed down is one way to create a more cycle-friendly environment.

In 2004, Rod King, who now runs 20splentyforus, cycled to Hilden in Germany to see how they had achieved a situation where 24% of all in town trips were done by bike. He expected to find a town with an integrated network of cycle lanes, but discovered it had been achieved simply by reducing the local speed limit to 30kph (about 18.6mph) in the 1990s. Towns like Portsmouth, Oxford, Norwich and Hull have now introduced 20mph on residential streets. It is too soon to assess the impact fully, but in Hull's 20mph zones, child pedestrian casualties have dropped by 74%. The existing default of 30mph is a relic from the 1930s when there were only 1.5 million cars on UK roads. Today, there are 33 million.

Portsmouth – the statistics	
Cost of implementing 20mph scheme:	£475,000
Number of roads covered:	1,200
Number of traffic orders needed:	6
Completed in:	9 months
Percentage of people questioned who wanted a 20mph speed limit:	80%

Engaging the local population was crucial. Public debate and consultation with local people allowed them to see the benefits (a quieter, safer street for them and their families) and take ownership of the project. Furthermore, lowering urban and residential speed limits to 20mph has been found to increase a 15-minute car journey by just 60 seconds.

In 2009, Islington Council was the first London borough to announce that all residential roads will be subject to the driving restriction by the end of the year. The initiative is likely to be introduced across other boroughs, but each local authority will have to make its own decisions, so local campaigning is critical. Living Streets, one of the charities behind the National Walk to School campaign, has welcomed calls to reduce the speed limit around schools to 20mph.

However, the most popular option at the time of writing is to opt for a variable 20mph limit operating only on school days at times when children are arriving at and leaving school. Generally, the position of existing school warning signs is taken as the most suitable distance for the starting and finishing points for the speed reduction. Solar-powered electronic flashing signs are an option although some schools prefer the more personal touch with signs designed by the children themselves. In each 20mph zone in Kingston upon Hull, the local schoolchildren get to paint a picture that is displayed below the 20mph warning sign.

FACT! *In areas where 20mph zones have been established, the number of children injured when either walking or cycling, has been reduced by 70% .[37]*

More car-free access points to the school

There are often little-used rear entrances to schools. Opening them up can, in some circumstances, mean a much shorter walk or bike ride to school. Card readers can deal with any associated security measures that are needed. Furthermore, new pedestrian-only entrances can raise the profile of walking and be much more welcoming. Before we started our project locally, one school had entrances that were shared between cars and children and were, frankly, unsafe. Now there is a smart new entrance exclusively for pedestrians, leading to a (literally) green path, which winds through the senior school to the junior school.

Cycle lanes

Dedicated cycle lanes are obviously the ideal solution for safe cycling, but, in the inner city at least, roads are often too narrow to accommodate them. Some campaigners also argue that cycle lanes are not there to help cyclists but to enable the cars to go faster without worrying about hitting cyclists, which means they can still endanger pedestrians. Some roads can be made safer for cyclists by introducing speed control and traffic calming measures. However parents I have spoken to would be much keener to let their children cycle to school if they did not have to share the road with drivers. Cycle lanes are expensive to install, but if there is potential for them in your area it is worth exploring possibilities with the local council. There are several types of cycle lane. They are:

• Mandatory cycle lanes: Marked by a solid white line or kerb edge. Other vehicles are not allowed to enter them;

• Advisory cycle lanes: Marked by a broken white line. Other vehicles can enter them but only when it is safe;

---

[37] *Transport Research Laboratory*

• Cycle lanes shared with pedestrians: Shared footways often with delineated cycle and pedestrian areas.

Advanced stop lines, painted boxes on the carriageway forward of the stop line, can sometimes be found at at signalised junctions. They allow cyclists to wait at the front of traffic and in full view of drivers, making it easier and safer to ride onwards or make a turn.

How to get a cycle lane installed

Talk to your local authority

The first thing you should do is check if your local authority is already planning to build a cycle lane where you want one. Many local authorities have a cycling officer, occasionally cover walking too, situated in one of these council departments: transport; highways; roads; traffic management; leisure or tourism. If your idea is already in the local plan then the new cycle lane may require no more effort on your part. However a local transport plan is only a framework and its implementation is not guaranteed, so you may still have to do some lobbying.

If your cycle lane proposal is not in the local plan, the local authority may still take up your suggestion, but you may need to lobby for your idea to be accepted. Certain factors may reinforce your bid, such as if there are other schools nearby whose pupils could also benefit from a cycle route.

Join an established cycling campaign or start your own

The Cycle Campaign Network is a national federation of UK campaign groups. Its members include groups such as the London Cycling Campaign, an umbrella group with several affiliates and Spokes, the Lothian Cycle Campaign. Another UK resource for cyclists is the CTC, the UK's national cyclists' organisation.

When you are part of an established group the council may consult you on road proposals or arrange a forum which meets a few times a year. Start a petition and get local support. Contact your councillor. He or she is there to represent you at local council level. There may be other councillors who are sympathetic to your cause. Attend council meetings when cycling is on the agenda.

Talk to Sustrans

If your cycle route is not on the local transport plan you may want to contact Sustrans, the national charity that supports sustainable transport nationwide, in partnership with local authorities and communities. Sustrans tries to link the National Cycle Network (NCN) with as many routes to school as possible and provides a child-friendly approach to increasing cycling in schools through the 'Bike It' scheme.

Sustrans has a public information line: 0845 113 0065.

MAKING A DIFFERENCE WITH A NEW CYCLE PATH - St Wilfred's School, Ashley Primary School and Margaret Sutton School in South Shields

Working with Sustrans, a new traffic-free link was created from the National Cycle Network that served all these schools.

Following completion, trips by children walking and cycling to school more than doubled from 79,000 to 161,000 per year.

Children also use the route heavily outside school hours (191,000 trips a year).

Finally many schools, especially in towns, are surrounded by streets that are too narrow to allow cycle lanes. The only solution here is to campaign for 20mph zones. This measure has been shown to reduce the accident rate significantly and makes cyclists feel much safer.

Pupils at Shawlands Primary School school say thank you for their zig-zag lines.

Photo courtesy of Ian Watson,, Glasgow City Council.

Pupils from Killylea School, Northern Ireland in their decorated wellies.

Photo courtesy of Margaret Kelsall, Killylea School.

Pupils tracking their progress on a virtual biking/walking tour of Sweden.

Photo courtesy of Hans Lindberg.

Chapter Six

**How to tackle the challenge
of changing behaviour**

How to tackle the challenge of changing behaviour

In my experience this is one of the biggest challenges. People may understand that their child needs daily exercise, they may appreciate the threat of climate change, but they don't want to be the ones to change their own personal behaviour.

There is hope. According to Prof. Steve Stradling, psychologist at the Transport Research Institute, Napier University, Edinburgh, about half of Scottish drivers want to cut their car use. In *Public Perceptions of Travel Awareness 2005* he identifies four driver groups:

• Die hard drivers;

• Complacent motorists - less attached to motoring, but see no reason to change;

• Malcontent motorists who find driving stressful and want to cut their car use, but can't see how, particularly in rural areas;

• Aspiring environmentalists who actively try to cut their car use.

Your School Travel Plan needs to come up with cost effective alternatives which will target the right driver group and level of thinking. Evaluating options for travelling needs to take into account the motivations of parents who drive to school and work out what will trigger different behaviour. A Scottish study[38] came up with the following classifications:

• Trip chainers – who are in the car on the way to somewhere else. Trigger for change is not easy – will have to be part of a bigger change process;

• Mother Hens – who don't feel their child is ready to face the world on their own. Trigger may be to appeal to the nurturing instinct and to emphasise the health benefits;

---

[38] *Why Do Parents Drive Their Children To School? Transport Research Series, Scottish Government*

• Security Conscious – who cannot accept that their child may be in more danger in the car than out. Trigger may be stressing the importance of building their child's life skills;

• Guilt Ridden – sees the car trip as giving them quality time with their child. Trigger could be health benefits or messages about better quality time;

• Duty Trips – feel taking their child in the car validates their role helping their child. Trigger may be to demonstrate that enabling the child to use other forms of transport makes them an even better parent;

• Only Hopes – who maintain there is no alternative to the car for their child. Trigger may be encouraging mixed methods of travel (Drive and Drop) and demonstrating advantages for both the child and the parent.

Ideally one would wish for personalised travel planning, but the STP can at least clarify choices for groups of parents and children - not just the bus/train routes, but also the times and cost on both outward and a choice of return journeys.

It is critical to demonstrate simply and clearly the benefits of initiatives and to reinforce their positive aspect rather than to dwell on the negative aspects of 'inappropriate' behaviour that attempts to create guilt in the minds of parents. Adopt the carrot not the stick approach.

You might need to help for parents find a lift-share partner is required as many parents are not awake to change or are too busy or lazy to investigate it seriously. Your STP will make it easier for discontented drivers to change. There is also a right time in terms of life events. When people have children starting at a new school they are ripe for transport messages.

PUTTING GREEN TRANSPORT AT THE HEART OF THE SCHOOL'S ETHOS - The Godolphin and Latymer School

Look at the homepage of this secondary school's website and you will see 'Travel to and from School' on the main menu. Follow the link and you are taken to local maps showing walking and cycling distances of 10 and 20 minutes from school. These allow parents to see easily if their daughter could consider walking or cycling. Other information includes the transport strategy and targets for the school. Deputy Headteacher, Emma Gleadhill, commented: "On open evenings for new parents and children we display maps showing where all the new girls live. In that way, some girls can see that they can walk or cycle and parents are less nervous about those living further away buddying up to come on public transport together."

Since the original travel plan was completed in 2006, the school has seen a 10% increase in girls walking to school.

You may have seen those little signs in hotels asking guests to save the planet and the laundering by letting the hotel know if they don't want towels to be replaced every day. The success rate is immeasurably improved if the hotel uses phrases like, 'We find that our guests want to help us save the planet.... People like you who have stayed in this room have hung up their towels because they care about our planet....' People are by nature conformist and want to do (and be seen to be doing) what others are doing. They are more likely to adopt behaviours that conform to that of their neighbours or peer group.

So when I speak to new parents at school events, I don't use directive language, which tells them what they should and shouldn't do. I simply suggest that this is a school that aims to teach their children important values about respecting others and respecting the planet ...and for that reason 'we find that parents at the school want to do their bit to try to avoid using their car to get to school'.

Habits are adopted very quickly so the more useful information that can be distributed before the child starts school, the better.

SITE SPECIFIC TRAVEL GUIDE - Steiner School, York

Anna Semlyen, author of the brilliant handbook Cutting Your Car Use, created a site-specific travel guide for her child's school, York Steiner School. It contains directions to school by non-road transport means, a specially-made map,, details on all the travel modes, bus, park and ride, car sharing etc, even buggy parking and useful phone numbers, websites, discounts for children etc.

Other measures to improve travel to the school included the installation of covered and lockable bike parking areas (the STP was required to secure funding); the creation of a safe; surfaced walking route to the entrance; formalised parking areas for staff and the introduction of a no-stopping zone on the lane approaching the school. A new entrance that allowed bikes and children to enter clear of a blind corner was also created and later widened.

Since these improvements, the number of children cycling has gone up from 19% to 25%.

Ideally, you will include details of other children travelling from their area and existing walking buses. But above all the school needs to stress the health benefits: we are a healthy school and it is as important for your child to walk to school as it is to eat a good breakfast or to get a good night's sleep.

The power of TV and campaigns like the 'clunk click every trip' and the moon-walking bear in TfL's 'watch out for cyclists' advert should not be underestimated. What is needed is significant investment to establish large-scale behaviour change programmes across the UK, tailored as much as possible to individual circumstances. The cost of such interventions would be dwarfed by the savings in ongoing costs to the NHS and society generally of ill-health and premature death.[39]

---

[39] TDavis, A, Valsecchi,C, and Fergusson, M. (2007) *Unfit for Purpose: How Car Use Fuels Climate Change and Obesity,* IEEP, London

Chapter Seven

How to communicate the message

Morton Way Song

Cheer:
Morton Way, let's walk to school
Morton Way, we know it's cool
Morton Way, let's Go for Green
And Morton Way, let's be seen!

Chorus:
Let's walk to school
Cause we know it's cool
Let's Go for Green
And let's be seen.

Verse 1:
There're butterflies and birds in the air
Keep on walkin' and they'll still be there
Walk to school and skip the car
Walk to school cause it's not too far.
Chorus

Verse 2:
Walk when you can and stay in shape
Breathe clean air and you'll feel great
Come on Morton Way, let's walk to school
Look after our health, that's the golden rule.
Chorus

Verse 3:
Keep on walkin' cause it's good for you
Keep your body active and feelin' like new
Get some exercise and always play smart
Let's walk Morton Way, you know it's good
for your heart.
Chorus

Verse 4:
Walk to school and walk to win
Check out the cleaner air and breathe it in
The streets are much safer when all of us walk
We'll be with our friends and we can talk.

Chorus—Cheer—Chorus

Morton Way Walks To School song,

written and composed by Cathy Clark (teacher and former parent council member at Morton Way P.S, Canada).

How to communicate the message

From the time you set up a working group to write a school travel plan, it is important to get key messages across to different audiences. You will need help and support and the more people know about the aims and objectives of the project the better. Here are some ways to keep parents, teachers, pupils, governors, staff at the local authority and local residents informed about the school travel plan, travel choices, meetings and events and achievements.

USING THE LOCAL MEDIA - Linköping, Sweden

An eight-week project focused on 10 to 13-year-olds. During the project, the pupils recieved extra lessons and information on different aspects of traffic and road safety. A big local media campaign was run at the same time. The pupils' bicycles were inspected and stickers with "safe bicycle" were awarded to pupils whose bicycles fulfilled road safety requirements. They also got information on how short car trips affect the environment, and on the importance of daily exercise. Every fortnight, the class's total distance of cycling and walking was registered on a very large world map. The pupils were thereby able to see how far they had moved during the period. The aim was that Linköping's 10 to 13-year-olds would cover as great a distance as possible during the course of the project. Eighteen schools and about 2,500 pupils participated, making it the largest cycle project which had been carried out in a Swedish town and one of the biggest in Europe. Hans Lindberg, project manager said: "It was amazing to see that these short distances turned out to be such an enormous distance when they were added together. The pupils walked and biked 132,090 kilometres during eight weeks. If the pupils, instead, had been taken by car, more than 31 tons of carbon dioxide would have been emitted." The funding for this project came from local councils, as well as the European Union.

According to surveys, the number of car journeys decreased by approximately 40%.

Existing channels

Offer to write a regular piece for the weekly school newsletter, encourage the school to include a section in the school magazine, in the school prospectus and on its website. See if it is possible to use an area on the notice board to keep people informed of progress. DUCKS nursery school in Dulwich, London, used red paper for their regular newsletter (see Appendix Four) to bring it to the attention of parents. Discuss with your local council its involvement in promoting key health benefits of leaving the car at home. Some, like Lambeth Council in London, are producing promotional literature and distributing it via GP surgeries and leisure centres.

New channels

• Dedicate a new school travel notice board to reports on progress and activities. Use visuals like maps to get the message across;

• Get agreement from the school to have a link on the school's website to a page on travel options;

• Provide information to parents that compares walking/cycling times with other modes of travel, remembering to allow for waiting times in the event of missing a bus or the time needed to find a parking space;

• Display this information using a local map with concentric circles radiating from the school location which indicate the housing within 5, 10, 15 and 20 minute walks or bike rides from the school;

• Get agreement for a parent-manned information stand at parents' evenings;

• Involve pupils in creating a logo for your school's travel plans to be used in any promotional materials;

• Work with pupils to produce their own illustrated newsletter on school travel issues. Consider whether key messages need to be translated into other languages for homes where English is not the first language.

Beyond the school playground

Getting a story into the national press is ambitious unless you have a serious accident or an established journalist among your parents, but the local press will often be interested in good stories about schools and innovative approaches. The combination of young people, environmental issues and the local community can often be enough to get their attention. Do some research not only on local newspapers and local radio/TV but also on which free magazines are distributed in the area and which community groups (local residents associations etc) produce publications and newsletters. Find out when their deadlines are. These are all possible vehicles for your stories. Positive media coverage will encourage more parents and pupils to get involved. Once you have your contact list

• Write your own press release using the school logo. Include positive quotes from pupils, parents and teachers (with their permission);

• Ring the journalist first to sell the story and follow up with a press release by email. Attachments can get spammed so include the text in the body of the email;

• Always write with simple, clear language covering the key aspects (what, why, where, how and who);

• Provide photos or suggest photo opportunities, ideally with pupils;

• Show the link between your activities and national campaigns such as Walk to School weeks etc;

• Develop and maintain a list of journalists with an interest in this theme;

• Never bother ringing local radio during the few minutes around the hour and half hour as they will be preoccupied with the news bulletins;

• Identify someone to take responsibility for co-ordinating publicity and responding to media enquiries. Include their name on every press release to develop continuity;

• Identify a parent or pupil who is skilled in photography;

• Consider carefully the image that is being presented in photos. Consider age, gender and ethnicity and if bicycles feature, check if the pupils are wearing helmets, reflective clothing etc in accordance with your school policy;

• Use any contacts you have to identify a local celebrity who might be persuaded to act as a patron and be quoted in press releases;

• If you have no luck with getting a story into the body of the paper, don't forget the letters page – after the TV listings, it is the second most read page of the paper.

Chapter Eight

How to involve young children in school - ideas for assemblies, clubs and classroom activities

How to involve young children in school - ideas for assemblies, clubs and classroom activities

Keeping the children involved is critical to the success of any STP project. Assemblies provide a great opportunity to talk to the teachers and children. After-school clubs provide a focus for children who might want to get more involved – and give them a taste for campaigning.

Assembly ideas

Kick off with a question for the adults present; ask how many of the teachers and parents present came to school by car when they were children. You will usually find that nearly all used to walk to school. Then ask the children who comes to school by car –very often you will be confronted with a sea of hands. Point out the difference and ask the children why they think there has been such a big change.

Focus on the positive aspects of alternatives to driving – ask the pupils how they would like to get to school and they will nearly always say 'by bike'. Ask them why and they will often emphasise the independence it gives them.

Follow up with questions about why it is important to think about leaving the car at home. Even very young children now have a sense of the damage that emissions do. See Appendix Five for a sample assembly.

After-school club ideas

If your school has clubs for different activities like swimming, dance, art etc, speak to the headteacher about running a club one afternoon a week. Here are some possible activities:

• Get the children thinking about why we should consider walking or cycling instead of driving to school;

• Go out onto local streets and do pollution tests on leaves in congested and quiet streets and compare the results;

• Prepare posters to put up round the school to promote walking/cycling to school. I made a massive banner with a group of children out of a spare roll of wallpaper. We laid it out in the classroom (holding down each corner). Then I poured some bright coloured paint onto a plate. Two brave children removed their shoes and socks and stepped in the paint. They then walked the length of the wallpaper, creating a random design of bare feet. It looked fantastic (though unfortunately it only lasted outside until the next downpour!);

• Prepare assemblies – get the children to act out getting to school by various different means and explain the associated consequences.

Classroom Activities

There is a plethora of resources on the internet for use in the classroom – a comprehensive database exists on the Department for Transport website[40], and the CTUK website[41]. Transport for London has also produced a large pack of resources linked to the National Curriculum.

Traffic Tamer Programme, Australia [42]

This is a grass-roots initiative powered largely by children. It teaches children the three magic ways to tame Dragon Wagons by changing their travel behaviour. Children earn Magic Stars each time they do something that helps make streets safer. For example, each time they walk to school they are resting their Dragon Wagon. The class is given a challenge collectively to earn a certain number of Magic Stars. When they reach this target, they are given a reward such as an extra break or a class party.

Organising street parties, writing adventure diaries and creating adventure trails are other ways in which the programme allows residents to reclaim the streets.

---

[40] http://www.dft.gov.uk/schooltraveldatabase/details.asp?ID=239

[41] http://www.cycletraining.co.uk/resources

[42] http://www.traffictamers.com

Geography

Encourage the children to do a virtual walk - individually or by class - to give them a sense of the surrounding geography and distances. They can start with a route from their home area to the nearest town centre, adding everyone's journeys into school on foot and plotting this on a chart on the wall. Once they have achieved the first destination they could then pick a town a bit further away and extend the total journey gradually. They could end up walking from London to Edinburgh or even from London to New York! Pupils can also survey and create maps for local walking/cycling routes to school.

BIKE AROUND THE WORLD

In 2009, the Sustrans Bike It project organised a 46,000 mile 'virtual' bike race around the world. Over 140 schools signed up to the race as a tool to promote cycling in their school. The race was inspired by the adventurer Alastair Humphreys, who spent four years doing the real thing. A DVD was produced and sent out to all the schools to be shown in assembly and inspire the children, parents and teachers to get their bikes out and join in the four-week virtual race.

In 2008, Sustrans organised a similar virtual bike race, the Tour D'Afrique which generated 30,000 bike journeys over the same period of time. Schools got miles added to their total each time a pupil, parent or staff member cycles to school. Each school had a notice board with a large map where the pupils and school community could follow the school's progress each day.

Some schools used the tour and Google Earth to study the geography of the areas they were passing through. Andy Casson of Sustrans highlighted the importance of people trying it for 4 weeks rather than just one day. "This type of challenge encourages every day cycling over four weeks; we have found it shows adults and children that cycling can just be part of their everyday life."

Maths

Keep logs of walking time or steps; calculate speeds and distances, individual and group averages, trends and statistical analyses (do boys or girls walk more?). Get the pupils involved in monitoring progress once the scheme is underway to see if children are changing modes of transport. The responsibility for counts on different modes could be rotated to different classes every term or year and pupils can organise the counts and analyse and display the results.

THOSE MILES REALLY ADD UP! - St Mary's Primary School, Northern Ireland

As part of a 'Walk around the world with Alastair Humphreys' project to motivate children to walk in, pupils had to calculate on a daily basis what distance everyone had walked or cycled. Pupils and staff taking part in the challenge earned virtual miles every time they chose to walk or cycle to school, which contributed towards their overall round-the-world total. They followed the route taken by Alastair Humphreys, the adventurer who cycled around-the-world in four years, and the winning school took just 8 days to complete the distance!

Science

Classes can look at ways of calculating pollution – even doing a simple test on tree leaves on busy and less busy streets highlights the issues clearly. In biology, there can be discussion about obesity issues. Research shows that a brisk one-mile walk to school takes about half an hour and can burn up to 150 calories. Use pedometers to measure steps, or simply measure walking time accumulated by students and study the health benefits of physical activity. Study the biomechanics of walking. For example, measure stride lengths - do they vary with height, weight, age, leg length? How does walking speed depend on your step speed and stride length? Look for specific plant or animal species, or make an inventory of indigenous species along walking routes. Catalogue seasonal changes in the flora and fauna. Older pupils can research the links between car use and climate change issues.

Art

Get pupils to design a poster promoting walking or cycling to school. Talk about the issues and run a competition to create a logo for the Safe Routes to School programme or to design a 20mph sign for the school.

GREENING THE TREES - *Bernadette Kowey, Program Co-ordinator, Vancouver, Canada*

This exercise is a creative way to survey the way your pupils travel to school.

"Draw a large tree with branches, but no leaves. This can be the class tree, but each child should draw their own tree as well. Every time a child walks or cycles the whole journey to school, they place a green leaf that they have created on their own tree and the class tree. A yellow leaf is used if they walk part of the journey or come by bus and a brown leaf represents a whole journey to school by car. Compare individual trees after several weeks. Which is the greenest?"

ARTY SIGNS - *Alleyn's Junior School, London*

Groundwork Southwark in London worked with the children in Year 4 to create designs for wooden plaques to promote sustainable travel. These were designed by the children, but carved by a professional and then installed around the neighbourhood to create a trail.

English

Create regular newsletters and write press releases to promote Walk to School Week. Write essays or keep a diary about the children's experiences of walking. Use the journey to school to inspire creative writing and get the children to think and write about transport patterns in the future and debate the pros and cons of different scenarios.

FABULOUS PACKS FOR TEACHERS IN LONDON - *Transport for London (TfL)*

TfL has produced a cycle curriculum pack for Key Stage 2, which is designed to complement the national literacy and numeracy strategies and History, Geography and DT QCAs. It includes the Lance Armstrong Biography, ballad poems by Mulga Bill, Tour de France number work, changes in bicycles since Victorian times, how to develop bike routes in the local area and how to design a cycling top. They are in the process of developing packs for Key Stage 3. The geography pack is already available with projects on the local community, learning from European neighbours and exploring links between local action and global impacts through the issue of car use.

History

Study historical locations in your community by walking to them. Talk to older members on the community about how they used to get to school.

Personal, Health and Social Education

Discuss with the children the issues around personal actions and how they affect the community and the environment. Give them the chance to take part in decision-making and to learn about the importance of citizenship.

Road safety features in the PHSE curriculum. The Good Practice Guidelines for Road Safety Education (DETR 1995) are based on extensive research for primary and secondary schools and provide examples of how to incorporate road safety education into the curriculum.

Information Technology

Ask pupils to design and create their own STP newsletter and get them to do some research on the web to find out what other schools are doing. Schools taking part in a SRS project can now use specially designed software and Ordnance Survey digital map data for their catchment area. By dragging and dropping symbols onto the computerised map, children can mark trouble spots, such as dangerous junctions and lonely or badly lit roads. By mapping their own routes, discussing problems and identifying potential solutions, more children will be encouraged to walk or bike to school. Parents can also be reassured that their children are safe and potential risk areas are identified and can be improved or avoided. Our local experience was that solid data can then be prepared and used to support bids to the local authority for funds to improve specific danger spots.

See www.ordnancesurvey.co.uk/education.

Design and Technology

Give the pupils an opportunity to design new facilities such as cycle racks or an interesting bike shed. Bike It officers have worked with primary school children to design and produce badges, sashes and even licence plates for their bikes – all with some reflective fabric to improve their safety. They worked with Charter secondary school in London to design and produce funky cycling clothing with teenage girls.

Music

Work with the children to compose rap songs along the theme of walking to school. These can then be sung as they walk into school.

Languages

Learn how to say 'I like to walk' in a language from each continent around the world! Create a link with a school in France (or another country), which is undertaking a similar project and exchange experiences. See www. mobilityweek.eu.

General Skills

The success of your school travel plan will be all the greater if the pupils are really involved and their work allows them to develop skills like problem definition, project management, leadership, public speaking, report writing and teamwork. All these skills are recognised as being important by universities and future employers, and can be included in UCAS forms as evidence of a broader perspective on life. If your school offers the Duke of Edinburgh Bronze, Silver and Gold schemes, find out if STP activities can count towards the service or skill element. Involve the pupils in:

• Consultation exercises with pupils and parents – they will use language that will produce better, more accurate responses from other pupils;

• Developing a display board and keeping it up to date with news;

• Keeping the school website up to date with news;

• Producing a regular newsletter;

• Making presentations at public meetings, to local councillors, MPs, assemblies;

• Organising events and fundraisers – they will know how to motivate other pupils to get them involved in Walk to School Weeks;

• Interviews for local papers. Help them prepare in advance with sample questions;

• Taking photos to be used for publicity;

• The STP working group – create links to the school council;

• Buddying schemes, where those with more experience of walking or cycling can help those with less experience. This is particularly helpful in the transition from primary to secondary school.

INTRODUCING THE SOCIAL ELEMENT - Morton Way School, Ontario, Canada

For pupils in this school, Wednesdays are 'walk to school' days and the older children in the environmental committee go into the classes to collect, tabulate and post the results throughout the school. The objective was to increase physical activity and decrease car drivers (normally between 60 -100 every day). On the first Wednesday of each month, parents and grandparents accompanying pupils to school are invited in to the school for coffee, conversation and a chance to sign back their children's library books. This helps to build a sense of community between the school and the families. A recent additional initiative to decrease car use further is the "25 cars or less" campaign. The number of cars dropping off children is monitored and a thermometer displayed to inform parents of the results. A PA system also announces the results to the pupils.

Surveys show that since the introduction of the initiative, between 89% and 95% of pupils walk on Wednesdays.

Councillor Lisa Rajan with pupils from St Joseph's Primary Catholic School with a globe symbolising the amount of CO_2 produced by the average car on the school run.

Photo courtesy of Southwark Council.

St Thomas of Canterbury RC School Car Free Day.

Photo courtesy of Richard Evans, Hammersmith and Fulham Council

Car Free Day Bike Parade in Portobello, Edinburgh.

Photo courtesy of Justin Kenrick

I walked to school!

Chapter Nine

How to exploit special days/weeks in the calendar to boost your campaign

How to exploit special days/weeks in the calendar to boost your campaign

Providing a focus for your project and linking up with other active schools in the area can encourage more parents and children to join in. Your local council should be able to provide you with publicity materials including posters and stickers to advertise the days/weeks concerned.

The UK Walk to School week takes place in May, the week before half term. The International Walk to School Month is in October, with thousands of schools around the world taking part.

Walk to School week and Walk to school month

The very first Walk to School week was in 1994, with just five Hertfordshire primary schools taking part. Today, almost two million children take part in the walk to school week in May (usually the third week) and in the walk to school month of October.

Each year there is a new theme to capture the imagination of the children: the fun and friendship that walking enables; health advantages; adventure and independence; and links between car travel and pollution. In 2009, pupils were encouraged to 'Walk 'n' Talk' on their way to school to experience the social aspect that walking together has for individuals and communities.

The first rule for an effective walk to school week is START PLANNING EARLY!! You can never have too much time to organise rotas of parents and volunteer helpers. The appendices contain proformas for letters to parents and newsletters. The basic aim should be to see how many children you can persuade to try an alternative to driving to school. To help parents who live too far to walk you could experiment for a week with various drop off points for Drive and Drop routes.

Parents and teachers are all busy people so start involving them at the beginning of the spring term in planning. Get the teachers to think about how they can incorporate some discussion of school travel into their lessons in Walk to School week. Ask the head teacher if one of the parents can work with some children to produce an assembly. Print a "Can you spot?" sheet for children to note what they see along the route (squirrels, dogs, letterboxes, taxis). Suggest that the school car park be closed for the day so the teachers can provide an example to the children.

CREATE YOUR OWN SPECIAL DAY - Deanery C of E Primary School, Sutton Coldfield.

Mark Cadwallader, deputy head, praises the fantastic efforts of a parent and teacher group who dreamt up a Green Day in June last year. Lots of fun environmentally-friendly activities were included and there was a major focus on transport. Families were encouraged to leave their cars at home through a novel approach; at least ten teachers were stationed around the school at various points past which the children would walk, some near the school and some further away. On the day, pupils could pick up a sticker from each teacher they passed. Some got up especially early and did a massive detour to get more stickers! These could be exchanged at school for healthy drinks and given to the teacher to prove how far they had walked. "It made both parents and teachers realise that walking was quicker than they thought and the road in front of the school was completely devoid of cars," said Mark. "The school participates in national walk to school weeks but having their own special day has made a big long-term impact."

79% of parents said that the STP had made them change their school travel habits.

The school has seen a 12% reduction in cars arriving at school and an 11% increase in walking.

Incentives

The STA at your council will be happy to provide packs including stickers, posters and charts to motivate the children. We have always found that incentives help children to persuade their parents to get involved.

Sweets

One year, all those walking into school were asked to bring in a sweet.

These were dropped into a transparent jar on the way in. By the end of the week it was full and the children had a competition to guess the number of sweets in the jar. The winner got to share them out among his/her class.

Marathons

Another year children were encouraged to predict how many miles or kilometres they thought they could walk or cycle. They logged their progress daily and at the end of the week the teachers helped them to calculate the total and see how many marathons each class had completed. In this way, children were encouraged to contribute to a team effort and the target in the first year, for each class to walk a marathon was easily met. In the following year nearly all classes walked more than 55 miles, with the winning classes reaching in excess of 75 miles in the week.

Challenge another local school

The following year – for extra motivation - we introduced some gentle, but inspiring competition with another local primary school to see which school could walk the furthest, expressed as an average per child. This helped to inspire community wide participation. The total for one school was 2.8 miles and for the other 2.6 miles in the week and the losing school was determined to win back the cup the following year.

Trainers

A popular incentive introduced by a rural primary school was to allow children to wear trainers if they walked or cycled into school – if that wasn't enough, they were even offered hot dogs on arrival.

Golden Shoe

Take an unwanted trainer, spray it gold and present it to the class with the most walkers/cyclists.

Raffle tickets

Other schools have given a raffle ticket to each child who walks or cycles. At the end of the week there is a draw and the winning child gets a prize (with luck, a bike donated by a local bike shop).

Cinema tickets

In New Zealand, SKYCITY cinemas provided tickets as rewards for participating in walk to school activities.

Balloons symbolising reduced CO2 emissions

A few years ago, Living Streets helped children to learn about the effects of greenhouse-gas emissions and the value of walking or biking to school by using large balloons to show how much carbon dioxide is emitted during a car trip to school.

Countdown timetable to Walk to School Week

• Spring PTA meeting – raise WTS week and discuss what your school could do;

• Gather together representatives of interested parties (parents, teachers, local council etc) to work out what is feasible;

• Identify possible Drive and Drop drop off points;

• Plan an after-school club for first half of summer term to work with children on assemblies, posters, banners etc.;

• In the summer term, contact local press to see if they are interested in doing a piece on your school;

• Contact the local council and/or www.livingstreets.org.uk and www. walktoschool.org.uk to order resources (stickers, charts, posters);

• Late April – send out information to parents explaining options and asking for volunteers for one week only;

• Early May – send out a reminder in the newsletter or ideally in a separate sheet confirming the Drive and Drop options available, encouraging parents to try biking, lift shares or just parking the car a bit further away from the school to allow their child to contribute to their class's total - DO STRESS THAT THE EVENT IS NOT ANTI-CAR. (see Appendix Six);

• Make sure you have enough volunteers on the day to help hand out stickers – involve the older children in these activities.

In 2008, the week coincided with Noise Action Week, and the focus was on traffic noise. Schools, parents and children were asked to be "Sound Detectives" - and enjoy all the sounds they wouldn't ordinarily hear if they were travelling to school in a car. Classroom materials are available every year from Living Streets.

Car-Free Day (In Town Without My Car)

September 22 is designated each year as World Car-free Day. Every year, road closures and other events are organised in towns and cities across the world including London and the UK. The day falls within the European Mobility Week.

By closing a road to motor traffic for the day, it is possible to get a glimpse of how life would be improved with less noise and air pollution. The road becomes a lively, convivial spot to spend the day, with on-street cafes, performances and other activities instead of the usual traffic. Schools can organise their own Car Free Day activities. For inspiration and ideas see www.dft.gov.uk/ itwmc

*In **Kingston, Surrey**, in 2008, part of a rat run outside a school was closed to traffic and transformed into a green, social space to show*

how different life could be. Cars and vans were replaced with a green area for outdoor lessons, music and fun activities for pupils. Activities included three pledge trees and a pledge leaf rubbing workshop, environmental workshops, road safety activities. After school, parents and residents were invited to join in the fun with an outdoor tea party, wacky races, pledging, Dr Bike, bike security marking, comedy unicycle theatre and a singer.

Shawlands Primary School in Barnsley *used the day in 2007 to say a big 'Thank You!' to parents for not parking on the School Keep Clear markings. A subtle way to promote the message that the council's parking attendants would be issuing fixed penalty notices to any vehicles parked illegally.*

In **Hammersmith and Fulham,** *the council signed the traffic order and delivered a car free street for 21 September. Activities on the day were organised by the staff and children of the St Thomas of Canterbury RC School. A 20mph poster competition and a street party made the children's day.*

In 2008, children at **Towerbank Primary School in Portobello, Scotland,** *participated in a workshop on the Friday afternoon to dress up their bikes for a parade along the prom and back up the High Street to the local market.*

Freewheel (London Only)

Nobody who has taken part in this car-free event will ever forget the sheer delight on the faces of all those who take advantage of this opportunity to reclaim the streets of central London by cycling down the Mall or along the Embankment with friends and families. My 10-year-old daughter biked up from Peckham Rye with some friends on one of the London Cycling Campaign-led rides. They felt completely safe riding over Southwark Bridge and practising bike tricks. The date in September has become a firm fixture in the calendar. Check the date, advertise the event in your school newsletter and get a team of children (and teachers!) along. They will be hooked for life.

Bike Week

Bike Week is held in June each year and is the UK's annual celebration of cycling. Dozens of rides and events are organised across the country, most of which are free to enjoy. It is a great opportunity to explore some of the rides available across the UK. See http://www.bikeweek.org.uk/

Events include:

• Rides suitable for everyone, including families, occasional cyclists and road bike enthusiasts;

• Bike2work, commuter challenge events and commuter breakfasts;

• Maintenance workshops, information campaigns and cycling festivals in different towns.

Walk on Wednesdays or Walk Once a Week (WOW)

This scheme was initiated by the Walk to Schools campaign in 2004 with the idea of introducing children and parents to the idea gradually and in an unthreatening way.

 FACT! In London WOW has increased the number of children walking to school by 30% [43]

The advantage is that it does not treat walking to school as something unusual, but simply as something that can easily be incorporated into people's daily lives. According to the Walk to School website, more than 30,000 children take part in the scheme nationally.

Resources are available from local councils to monitor children who are taking part in the scheme and there are incentives such as stickers and badges to provide extra encouragement.

---

[43] *http://www.walktoschool.org.uk*

WE LOVE WOW - *Dulwich College Junior School, London*

Camilla Mair and Karen Jones, who have introduced the WOW scheme at Dulwich College Junior School, said: "A few parents objected and told us to stop telling them how to run their lives but on the whole the reaction has been very positive. The support from the council has been great; the scheme is so simple and really appeals to the children, who love collecting the stickers and badges. Since kick-off four months ago, it has snowballed, with the formation of informal groups of walkers and parents taking turns to share the load of transporting musical instruments etc. The main thing is that WOW makes sure that children who are walking are very visible to the other children who then want to join in."

Chapter Ten

How to get funding and other support

How to get funding and other support

What you need to know – and whom you need to influence

The local authorities highway department is responsible for maintaining roads in a given area. Funding to make infrastructure changes identified in the STP is available through the Local Transport Plan process. Funds for changes as outlined in chapter 5 do not go directly to the school, but are spent by the highways departments on projects that will benefit the schools. Generally the highway authority will be your local council but if you live in a parish or town council area you will need to refer to the county council. A quick check of the local council website can tell you who is responsible for roads in your area.

It is essential to understand the local and national government departments that can be of use to you in your attempts to change transport habits locally. What follows is a brief summary of a situation that is constantly changing. You are advised to consult the relevant websites (see Appendix One) to establish the existing situation.

There are three layers in the overall structure:

National government departments

Department for Transport, Department for Children, Schools and Families, and Department for Health are of relevance to Safe Routes to School projects. The first two departments share responsibility for the management of the STP project through the Travelling to School Project Board. The 2006 Education and Inspections Bill establishes a statutory responsibility for local education authorities to 'assess the school travel needs of their area and to promote the use of sustainable modes of transportation.[44]

Regional government

Regional school travel advisers are responsible for managing the Travelling to School project at regional level and act as a channel for information between

---

[44] *Information Report on Cross-Boundary Links and Meeting Local and National Targets on Children's and Young People's Issues, p3 Education and Inspections Bill*

134 published 28 February 2006

the local STAs and the national civil servants. In London, the metropolitan bodies like the Greater London Authority and Transport for London are valuable sources of funding.

Local government

This is your first port of call. All local authorities (also known as highway authorities when dealing with transport issues) must have a Sustainable Mode of Travel Strategy (SMoTS) which should be published and should include targets for increasing cycling and walking. In London any money from TfL comes through the local council. Also in London the local implementation plan (LIP) sets out how the council will work with partners over the coming years to co-ordinate and improve its transport services. Local councils vary significantly in their approach to sustainable school transport. The Department for Transport gives each local authority an annual allocation of money to carry out the transport projects in its local transport plan. The local authority then decides which projects it can afford to fund. Money from other government departments may also be channelled through the local authority.

State schools who submit their school travel plans will be given capital grants for projects such as bike racks, lockers etc. At the time of writing, this amount is £3,750 per nursery/primary school plus £5 per pupil and about double that for secondary schools. This money comes from the Department for Children, Schools and Families and is paid direct to schools. In London, this is available until the end of 2009, and in the rest of the country until the end of 2010. TfL tops up the money to provide the same grant to independent schools in London.

How the School Travel Advisers can help – hints and tips

In my experience STAs are often underappreciated and overwhelmed by a massive burden of work from demanding schools and councils. Here are a few tips:

• Identify a parent or teacher who can act as a school champion;

• Work towards ownership by the school community and also involve the wider local community;

• Focus on just a couple of promising schools so their positive experience can be used as an example to the others;

• It is best to start at the beginning of the academic year to allow a full school year to complete the plan;

• Keep the process as simple as possible – short and snappy surveys;

• Don't let the school travel plan sit on the shelf once complete – get started on actions as soon as possible;

• Ensure all your local schools are fully aware of what is on offer from the council (stickers, badges etc);

• Exploit all the resources in your council (GIS experts, parking officers, traffic engineers);

• Maximise all local media opportunities to draw more schools into the project;

• Get good communication links in place with relevant councillors;

• Use the PLASC data to identify the baseline situation and use mapping software to bring it alive for the schools. Don't get put off by concerns over data protection – this depersonalised data so no-one can be identified;

• Link the STP project with others like the Healthy School Programme, which have overlapping goals;

• Recognise the synergies of working with neighbouring schools. Otherwise solving one school's problem may create issues for the other.

Transport for London – www.tfl.gov.uk

The local group that I helped to set up has found TfL to be very responsive to our requests for funding to improve the local infrastructure. Over about five years our group obtained more than £250,000. This was only because school travel plans were drawn up and clear targets for improvement (new zebra crossings, traffic lights etc.) identified. There is an enthusiasm to make it easier for children to walk or bike to school but the officials are not on the spot and cannot know exactly what is required. Any approach to them has to be via your School Travel Adviser and you have to have a school travel plan to back up your request for funding.

In the past, campaigners had to work with their local council to bid for lots of small schemes, but from April 2010 the money that TfL distributes will be in much bigger packets with a lot more flexibility. This will mean that you will have a much better chance of bidding for larger schemes to transform the area around your school for the better.

TfL also has a role promoting Junior Road Safety Activity packs and curriculum resources are available for pupils once the school has registered with it.

Council officers and staff

We found a wealth of experience and resources in our local council All councils now have at least one School Travel Adviser (STA) but there are other who could help, including:

- traffic team;

- cycle promotion officers;

- health promotion unit (and increasingly the Primary Care Trusts);

- education section especially those dealing with property;

- community safety team;

- health development officers;

- community planning and education centre;

• parking enforcement;

• lighting streets and signs;

• paving/kerb replacement or repair unit.

Local councillors are also often willing to get involved and support your case. A lot of funding decisions revolve around personal relationships so get to know the councillors who count in your borough. In Southwark, London, for example, in 2009, £300,000 was available through the 'Cleaner, Greener, Safer' scheme, which can fund physical changes to roads, pavements and cycle parking among other things. Access to this funding is through the eight community councils.

In addition, Primary Care Trusts are becoming more interested in funding activities that will show long term health benefits. Every PCT has a director of public health who has an interest in increasing the number of healthy active children in their area. In London, for example, physical inactivity costs about £3 million in each Primary Care Trust. Contact them through your local School Travel Adviser. The National Healthy Schools Programme is also relevant. This is a long-term initiative that aims to make a difference to the health and achievement of children and young people. The government has set a target that all schools will be participating by 2009.

To achieve Healthy School status the school must (as a minimum):

• be engaged with representatives from the Safe Routes to School programme and School Travel Plan (STP) scheme;

• have a STP in place or be working towards one;

• have given parents/carers information regarding the school travel plan via newsletter articles/letters and so on;

• have used school travel plan surveys to develop the broader physical activity agenda;

• promote walking and cycling to school all year round and in a planned way;

• make pedestrian and cycle skills training available for children, young people and staff.

Your local MP may also be helpful in supporting a particular campaign, especially if they have an interest in the environment, transport or education. Check www.parliament.uk to find out who your MP is and where their interests lie.

Other sources of funding could include: local charitable trusts; national charitable trusts; the National Lottery; and the European Commission public health section.

Working with business both local and national

Get people behind your local campaign and don't forget the support you can get from companies and shops in your area.

Our local bike shop, Edwardes of Camberwell, has always been keen to support our efforts with bike helmets and similar incentives for schoolchildren. Other companies that are trying to market to families are good targets for support. Insurance companies and local estate agents are often willing to pay for tabards if they can display their name on them prominently. Co-operative companies have a commitment to plough a percentage of their profits back into the community, so they are also candidates.

Any approach to a local company needs to identify the reasons why they should support you. These might include improving its profile and image in the local community, providing marketing opportunities among parents and children, promoting its green credentials and so on.

Asda Stores in Newcastle

Newcastle City Council negotiated an arrangement with Asda, which has a superstore within 200 metres of Gosforth East Middle and 400 metres of Broadway East First Schools. Parents may park in the store's car park and use a specially-created off-road path to the school. This benefits both the children and Asda.

The ideal approach is one made through a personal or professional link. Follow this up with face-to-face contact and a concrete, costed proposal where relevant. Consider the timing – towards the end of the financial year may be more productive.

Co-op Walking Bus packages

Is your school near a Co-operative Group store? Are you thinking of starting a walking bus?

If the answer to both questions is "yes", you may be eligible for one of their Walking Bus packages, which includes the following materials:

• *40 junior or infant high visibility (hi-viz) vests;*

• *10 adult hi-viz vests;*

• *Banner for the school railings, to promote the bus to children and parents;*

• *Posters for use in the school to promote the bus;*

•*50 hi-viz snapbands as rewards for the walkers.*

Identify large corporate companies in your area. Find out if they have CSR (corporate social responsibility) programmes and whether or not these could benefit your project. If they do, their employees will be encouraged to engage with the local community in voluntary activities. Identify areas where individuals or teams could contribute to your project teaching road safety, cycle training etc. The big advantage of these volunteers over parents is continuity. When one employee leaves a programme in place, he or she should be replaced by another volunteer.

CELEBRATING COMMUNITY CHAMPIONS - Smethwick and Pulborough Tesco Metros

Tesco has introduced Community Champions into 65 of their stores (and five distribution centres) with a view to extending the scheme to more stores over 2009. Community Champions support local initiatives, many of which are about safe cycling and walking. Smethwick and Pulborough Metro stores have supported local 'walking bus' initiatives, donating the day-glo tabards and providing a safe location (store car park) to start the walk. In winter, they have provided warm drinks and Smethwick donated a prize for the child who walks to school the most often. Ruth Girardet, Corporate Responsibility Manager, commented: "Tesco are committed to supporting the local communities around our stores. We know that cycling is an excellent way of getting fit and of cutting our carbon emissions, so we are delighted to support local safer cycling initiatives."

The future – an agenda for change

The future – an agenda for change

This book has been based on the experience of one small group of schools. The results in terms of modeshift were not dramatic. But at least we have reversed the trend and we are seeing improvements over the years, with more pupils taking up walking and cycling and parents starting to think twice before automatically driving their children to school.

How can we make sure that trend continues? Only through action by central and local government, by schools, parents and their children.

We need school travel to feature strongly in the climate change debate. We need it to feature in the obesity debate. If the government is serious about reducing the NHS bill and meeting environmental targets, a two-fold approach is needed; tools for schools and a shift in government mentality to make driving less attractive and walking/cycling more attractive.

Cities such as Bristol and Blackpool will hopefully benefit from the £100m worth of funding aimed at improving cycling infrastructure and promoting the benefits of cycling over the next three years. A recent government campaign includes measures to recompense overweight parents who walk their children to school with supermarket-style vouchers to spend on sports gear and healthy food. But this is all extremely piecemeal and sporadic.

Look at the homepage of the Department for Transport and you are confronted with four options: air, road, rail and sea! No option for walking and cycling. We need a radical shift in mentality to understand that walking and cycling are important. And it is critical that our children acquire this mentality from an early age. Only by making car ownership and use more expensive and less attractive can we decrease car use. Only by introducing fiscal measures designed to make sustainable modes of transport more competitive (such as a programme of incremental increases in fuel taxes) will the long-term trend of declining real costs of motoring be reversed. A lot of noise is made at the top about child safety, but government still fights shy of easy transformative measures such as the introduction of 20mph zones around every school. Because the government still sees anti-car measures as vote-losers it fudges the issue and offloads responsibility to the local level. Avoiding the issue by putting the idea of congestion charge zones to citizens of Manchester and Glasgow (both towns voted against it) is not acceptable. After all, turkeys don't vote for Christmas! If only they could adopt the approach of Barack Obama when he said just after his election: "Now is the time to make tough choices", before introducing measures to at last put the brakes on US gas guzzlers.

One of the buzz-words of the current Labour government is 'choice'. A minister spoke of the desire to go further and "present (parents) with a choice of good schools so that they can decide on the most suitable one for their child. At the moment choice is often only available to those who can afford it – those who can move house into their preferred school's catchment area or who can pay up for a private education. But I am determined to give more choice to those parents who can't afford these options"[45]. Is not the reality of parental choice an education system that brings with it more child miles and ever declining numbers of children walking and cycling to school?

Government has to get more serious about giving parents and teachers the tools to tackle the school run challenge. What is needed is significant investment to establish large-scale behaviour change programmes across the country. The cost of such progammes would be dwarfed by the savings in ongoing costs to the NHS and society. Research shows that for every £1 spent on smarter choices programmes, the benefit in terms of environment, congestion and public health could be as high as £10.[46] The recent changes in the Education and Inspections Act,[47] where local authorities now have to conduct needs audits and infrastructure audits to encourage sustainable travel will, one hopes, lead to a greater focus on this area. However, provision of STAs and support for STPs is only available from local councils until 2010, as things stand at the time of writing. This support also needs to be backed up by a solid set of options which schools can adopt. No two schools are the same – some will need help to encourage cycling, others to promote Drive and Drop and others will focus on walking to school. Existing levels of investment in walking and cycling in continental Europe run at about five times higher than in the UK.

---

[45] Jacqui Smith, 2006 at IPPR conference

[46] S Cairns, L Sloan, C Newson, J Anable, A Kirkbride and P Goodwin. Smarter Choices: Changing the way we travel, DfT 2004

[47] Education and Inspections Act 2006 – Home to School transport provisions

Teachers and schools already have too much on their plates. It is therefore critical that funding be extended and the STA positions made permanent to provide long-term support on school travel. Schools will only make progress if they maintain the momentum. Focusing on prospective and new parents is fundamental, because habits are formed very early on. Involving the pupils and embedding the work and practices into the school curriculum and school calendar is also critical. Other success factors include using benchmarks, setting realistic targets, monitoring progress, and constantly exploring new ideas and involving new parents in the project.

It is staggering how the car is still the unthinking default option for so many people – I was shocked to hear a member of the Safe Routes to School group suggest a new location for the regular meetings, adding that one advantage was very good car parking outside the venue!

There is still a lot of work to do. A lot can and must be done by central and local government and by the schools. But as parents we also need to think about changing our attitudes. If we want our children to grow into independent, grounded, responsible adults, we need to let go a bit. We need to give them the freedom to make mistakes, and to explore their neighbourhood. Only then will we create relaxed and friendly communities and streets full of people instead of cars.

I started this book by describing the joys of walking to school as a child. When I reflect on the seemingly uphill task of getting parents to leave the car at home, I think of how attitudes to, say, smoking have changed over the last 20 years and remind myself that every successful campaign started in a small way, with a few people. And reflecting on the highs and lows of the campaign over the years I remember how rewarding it has been to spend that half an hour with my children on the way to school. We complain about the time our children spend playing computer games and watching television... instead of being with their family. Getting into a regular routine of walking gives you time away from the TV and other distractions... time just to listen while your children are still young enough to want to talk to you. ....or simply to share the fun of watching a dog chasing a squirrel or to admire the cloud formations.

Go on...give it a go...you won't regret it!

Appendix One

Local, regional and national resources for your project

Local, regional and national resources for your project

The good news is that there is a wealth of help out there to support and encourage your group. The main players are listed below.

Local bike shops always looking for more trade can be helpful with local maps and with freebies like bike helmets and bike bells to give out as prizes.

Local council not only advice and guidance but also many goodies like reflective jackets, pedometers, motivational stickers.

WALKING

Living Streets – www.livingstreets.org.uk

This website should be your first port of call. It contains a mass of information on how to set up a Safe Routes to School project and works to encourage more people to walk and to ensure our streets are designed to allow people to do that. Their consultancy services support professionals, their campaigns encourage walking and they work to lobby opinion formers to put walking issues firmly on the front foot. Living Streets is also responsible for running the major national campaign called Walk to School (see below).

Step Up – www.stepup.org.uk

A campaign set up by Living Streets aimed specifically at secondary children to encourage them to walk to school. At the time of writing, only 41% of this group walked to school regularly so the challenge is to establish what the barriers are and how more walking can be encouraged. Activities include a competition to establish what teenagers think would transform their streets for the better and a code game to encourage walking.

Think Feet First – www.thinkfeetfirst.com

This a health initiative linked to the Change4Life campaign. Its website encourages the public to thinking about walking rather than using the car and it has launched hundreds of walking to health programmes. The emphasis is on fun. It provides hints and tips to enable families to change their lifestyle and get fit and active.

Walk to School – www.walktoschool.org.uk

The Walk to School campaign is run by the charity Living Streets with funding from Department for Transport and the Big Lottery fund. It asks parents, pupils and teachers to think about their journey to and from school and the many benefits of making it on foot.

About 50% of children don't walk to school regularly and more pupils are being driven to school in a car. This trend is contributing to reduced physical activity and increased childhood obesity, urban congestion and air pollution.

Each year, they organise two nationally recognised events: **International Walk to School Month** (October) and **National Walk to School Week** (May).

They want people to see walking to school as an everyday activity, so they also run the **WoW** (Walk Once a Week or Walk on Wednesdays) scheme, which rewards pupils with a collectible enamel badge if they walk to school regularly.

Walk England – www.walkengland.com

Walk England is a social enterprise that works in partnerships across the country to create local opportunities for people to choose to walk, to walk more often, to walk to more places, and to feel safe while doing so.

The Walk England website is one of a portfolio of projects being delivered by the Travel Actively consortium of the leading walking, cycling and health organisations in England.

Travel Actively is delivering 50 practical projects that will encourage people to travel actively for their health and well-being. It is hoped that two million people will become more physically active by walking or cycling as part of their daily lives by 2012.

CYCLING

Sustrans – www.sustrans.org.uk

Sustrans is the UK 's leading sustainable transport charity. Its vision is a world in which people choose to travel in ways that benefit their health and the environment, and every day the charity works on practical and innovative solutions to the transport challenges facing us all. Sustrans pioneered Safe Routes to Schools in the UK, and with Bike It and its work to build dedicated walking and cycling routes to schools, Sustrans is doing all it can to enable millions of children to walk and cycle the school run with an ambition to provide a safe route to school for every child in the UK.

Sustrans is also the charity behind the award-winning National Cycle Network and many other initiatives delivered in communities UK-wide to enable individuals to choose to walk, cycle and use public transport more and to re-design their streets to create more liveable neighbourhoods where children can play outside free from the fear of traffic. For more information on all of Sustrans' work, visit its website. If you like its aims, please do consider joining the charity as a supporter or volunteer.

Bikes and Trailers www.bikesandtrailers.com

Cycle trailer and trailer bike specialist.

CTC – www.ctc.org.uk

CTC is the country's largest group of people on bikes. Its mission is to make cycling enjoyable, safe and welcoming for all. Its work, which includes high-profile campaigning on behalf of all cyclists, is made possible by support from its members. The CTC guide to Family Cycling contains everything you need to know about cycling with children. The guide includes: How to teach your child to ride, what to look for when you buy a bike for yourself or your child, how to choose child-seats and trailers, and the best places to cycle with your family.

CTUK (Cycle Training UK) – www.cycletraining.co.uk

This company was established in 1998 to provide professional training in on-road cycling across London. it is the biggest independent provider of on-road cycle training and cycle maintenance training in London. It also trains instructors throughout the UK. Whether you've not ridden for years, never learned at all or want to ride more confidently – CTUK can help! It also provides tailor-made training for individuals and families, schools, workplaces, and local authorities.

Cycling England - www.cyclingengland.co.uk

Cycling England is a government-funded but independent, expert body, working to get more people cycling, more safely, more often. It promotes the growth of cycling in England by championing best practice and channelling funding to partners engaged in training, engineering and marketing projects. It constantly promotes cycling. Its contribution to Safe Routes to School is mainly in the area of training: showing how the humble bicycle can transform the way we travel to create a greener, healthier nation. According to its website, almost half of children would prefer to travel to school by bike, but only 2% do so.

Cyclescheme – www.cyclescheme.co.uk

This website adminsters a tax efficient scheme for employees to get up to 50% off the retail price of new bikes and cycle equipment. The remaining cost is deducted from the monthly salary, saving both the employer and the employee tax.

Dutchbikes – www.dutchbike.co.uk

Supplier of a range of great bikes for carrying children. Based in Cambridge but happy to deliver around the UK.

Go-Ride – www.britishcycling.org.uk/go-ride

Ever tried cycling around a proper velodrome? For me it was a real 'feel the fear and do it anyway' moment as I tried to get to grips with a bike going round a seriously sloping track with no brakes and no chance of freewheeling in Herne Hill! After the 2008 Team GB Olympic successes, there has never been a better time to encourage young people to extend their interests from cycling to school to more ambitious racing.

Go-Ride is British Cycling's Club Development Programme aimed at improving both young riders and clubs. It focuses on young members – improving coaching standards and increasing the number of young riders with access to coaching activities.

Go-Ride supports the creation of school-club links, which helps provide clubs with a constant influx of new young members and helps everyone work towards their shared vision of more young people, more active, more often in cycling. Look at the website to create a link between your school and a local Go-Ride community club.

Kinetics – www.kinetics.co.uk

Company selling electric bikes, scooters, trailers and folding bikes.

London Cycling Campaign – www.lcc.org.uk

LCC's vision is to make London a world-class cycling city. The key objectives are to improve the quality of life in London by increasing cycling, to involve people from all London's communities in cycling, to bring about the best possible services for people who want to cycle in London and to be at the forefront of research and policy linking cycling to wider issues.

The Community Cycling Fund for London (CCFL) project, funded by Transport for London, allows community groups to apply for up to £5,000 for cycling projects that will encourage, support and promote cycling in their community. In 2008, grants were allocated to more than 36 community projects in London.

It has a fantastic array of resources for everyday cycling, including a set of 12 information booklets about cycling, ranging from Buying a Bike and Getting Started to Cycle Security and Cycle Maintenance, which can be downloaded from its website. It also worked on the 19 London Cycle Guides produced by Transport for London to encourage more Londoners to choose cycling as their mode of transport. Get hold of copies to encourage parents to get their bikes out by ringing on 020 7234 9310.

There are also lots of local borough groups like Southwark cyclists, which organise masses of fun rides and can get involved in training children.

Parliamentary cycle group

The annual All-Party Parliamentary Bike Ride aims to promote cycling for all as part of the Bike2Work campaign. In 2007, it had a special Tour de France theme, which saw about 25 MPs and peers riding the route of the Prologue course (7.9km) of the Tour de France, including Tom Harris, Emily Thornberry, Adrian Bell and Richard Caborn.

Quicker By Bike – www.quickerbybike.com

A campaign to promote cycling to non-cyclists and decent cycling to existing cyclists. Information on how to commute by bike, great bike shorts with logos to encourage others onto their bikes.

Velorution Bike Shop - www.velorution.biz

Wonderful bike shop in London full of wacky and not so wacky bikes for individuals and families. Great website with inspiring images and information about cycling events.

CLASSROOM ACTIVITIES

BRAKE - www.brake.org.uk

This organisation campaigns for road safety, offers support to victims of accidents and conducts research.

Community mapping - www.communitywalk.com

This website links to Google maps and allows you to plot different locations providing you have the postcode. You can import up to 500 addresses from an excel file – very useful to show how close people live to school, to get an idea of good walking bus routes or for the young people to highlight areas of concern.

Department for Transport – www.dft.gov.uk

Lots of information on the website and some surprisingly cool graphics. The site includes a 'road safety game', which I couldn't work out and even my 12-year-old thought was impossible! However there is also a database of classroom materials relating to sustainable travel. The database is a catalogue of information on teaching and other relevant resources relating to encouraging greater use of walking, cycling, public transport and car sharing for school journeys.
http://www.dft.gov.uk/schooltraveldatabase

Eco-schools – www.eco-school.org.uk

The government in England wants every school to be a sustainable school by 2020. Eco-Schools is an international award programme that guides schools on their sustainable journey, providing a framework to help embed these principles into the heart of school life.

Eco-Schools is administered in England by ENCAMS; in Scotland by Keep Scotland Beautiful; in Wales by Keep Wales Tidy; and in Northern Ireland by Tidy Northern Ireland. It is now easy for Eco-Schools across the world to get in touch and explore ways of working together on environmental issues. Visit www.eco-schools.net to find instructions on how to register your school and carry out a search. After finding an Eco-School that matches your criteria, you can then contact the 'match' school by post, telephone or email.

Once registered, schools follow a simple seven-step process, which helps them to address a variety of environmental themes, ranging from litter and waste to healthy living and biodiversity. Children are the driving force behind Eco-Schools; they lead the eco-committee and help carry out an audit to assess the environmental performance of their school. Through consultation with the rest of the school and the wider community, it is the pupils who decide which environmental themes they want to address and how they are going to do it. Schools work towards gaining one of three awards, Bronze, Silver and the prestigious Green Flag award, which symbolises excellence in the field of environmental activity. Bronze and Silver are both self-accredited through this website and Green Flag is externally assessed by ENCAMS.

Schoolway - www.schoolway.net

Simple website for teachers and pupils that gives advice on best practice actions a school can take to improve the journey to and from school. It uses interactive ways to demonstrate what teachers can do in class to encourage an enjoyable, healthy, sustainable and safe way to school and inspire traffic education. It also offers children a chance to play the 'Traffic Snake Game' and includes a picture gallery showing other schools that have become involved.

Liveable Streets Education – www.streetseducation.org

This is a US website with news, activities and videos. It is also developing useful resources for teachers which will be available shortly.

Tales of the Road – www.talesoftheroad.direct.gov.uk

Road safety site for children with fun games, advice and competitions

GENERAL

20's Plenty For Us – www.20splentyforus.org.uk

This organisation was formed in order to campaign for the implementation of 20mph as the default speed limit on residential roads in the UK. Research has shown that the vast majority of the public would like 20mph on residential roads. Recent changes in Dept of Transport guidelines have relaxed the recommendations and in many residential areas 20mph limits may be set without any physical measures at all. The site shows how 20's Plenty saves lives, reduces accidents and makes very little difference to actual journey times.

Brightkidz – www.brightkidz.co.uk

Following problems identifying suppliers of high-visibility clothing that was appealing to school children, Alison Holland set up a social enterprise in 2004, which worked with children to come up with designs. The resulting clothes, bags and accessories are now sold to schools, local authorities, businesses and individuals throughout the UK and abroad.

Campaign for Better Transport - www.bettertransport.org.uk

Formerly called Transport 2000, this organisation provides national expertise that is described aptly on its website as informed and informing. Within the organisation, there are also local campaigners who are passionate, driven, and fighting for a better environment for all of us. Since 1973, it has been helping to create transport policies and programmes that give people better lives. Working nationally and locally, collectively and as individuals, through high-level lobbying and strong public campaigning, it makes good transport ideas a reality and stops bad ones from happening. It can support your school if there is a need to campaign against damaging road-building schemes or to help communities blighted by dangerous, noisy and polluting traffic.

Car-Free Day/Mobility week - www.mobilityweek.eu

In September most European cities and towns have the opportunity to participate in the most widespread event on sustainable mobility, the European Mobility Week. A full week of events dedicated to sustainable mobility is organised in more than 2000 cities and towns. This initiative has emerged from the concern of Europeans about pollution and urban mobility. In town, many people complain of a poor quality of life: air pollution, noise pollution, congestion, etc. And yet, the number of cars is increasing. Use this week to focus the children's attention on sustainable transport issues or, if a week is too long concentrate on 22 September, which is the European In Town, Without My Car! day, and now a firmly established date in the calendar of governments across Europe and beyond. On this day every year, town centre streets close to cars and lorries, and open up for people to enjoy walking, cycling, street theatre, live music, dancing, public art and children's play areas.

Children's Play Council - www.ncb.org.uk/cpc

Promotes home zones and safer streets.

Community Transport Association – www.communitytransport.com

Advice, information and training on running not-for-profit community transport like minibuses. Discounted vehicle purchase.

Department for Children, Schools and Families – www.dcsf.gov.uk

Resources and free guides including A Safer Journey to School and the Communications toolkit.

Groundwork UK – www.groundwork.org.uk

Groundwork works with children in and out of school to illustrate how individual actions can make a difference to the local and global environment. It teachs pupils about transport issues and helps pupils to understand the vital role they can play in reducing carbon emissions and saving resources.

Multimap – www.multimap.com

Like the TfL website, but national (and international). Provides walking directions but not cycling directions and also has weather forecasts.

Transport for London – www.tfl.gov.uk

This website will show you how to get from A to B by public transport and also by bike or on foot. Incredibly helpful and easy to understand maps can be downloaded and printed out. General information on transport, maps, guides and useful links.

Travelwise – www.travelwise.org.uk

ACT TRAVELWISE is a membership body for any organisation or person that is either developing or delivering a travel plan, a marketing campaign for changing travel behaviour, advising on sustainable travel initiatives or providing sustainable transport services to others.

The main benefit of membership is to network with travel planners and people involved in sustainable transport around the country, to share each others' experience, documents, pictures and ideas in order to further the collective knowledge and best practice in this fast emerging field.

Viewfinder - www.viewfinder.infomapper.com

Main purpose is as a tool for pupil survey (questionnaires and map-based survey), development and monitoring of school travel plans. Developed from the now defunct Young Transnet. Best bit of the site is the route plotting tool and lots of quick guides.

Appendix Two

The Science

The Science

The majority of parents, teachers and pupils do not need to be persuaded of the necessity to reduce their car use and try to find ways to leave it at home. However, there are always some exceptions so I have summarised briefly the arguments below.

It took more than 200 million years for the oil beneath the Earth's surface to form. In the past 200 years, we have already used half of that reserve. If current rates of consumption continue, the world's remaining oil will be used up in 40 years.

At the moment, two-thirds of the oil consumed around the world powers lorries and other vehicles, and half goes to passenger cars and small vans. Being conscious of our fuel use will help to conserve resources for future generations.

 FACT! Road transport is responsible for 22% of the UK's total greenhouse gas emissions.

Transport involves the combustion of fossil fuels to produce energy translated into motion. Pollution is created from incomplete carbon reactions, unburned hydrocarbons or other elements present in the fuel or air during combustion.
Typical vehicle emission pollutants include carbon monoxide, nitrogen dioxide, volatile organic compounds such as benzene and toluene, and tiny smog particles less than 2.5 microns in diameter. Exposure to these pollutants has been linked to diseases and adverse outcomes such as cancer, asthma, emphysema, leukaemia, reduced fertility and low birth-weight.

Cars also emit several pollutants classified as toxins, which cause as many as 1,500 cases of cancer in the country each year. Car emissions also contribute to the environmental problems of acid rain and global warming.

Pollution control measures have drastically reduced emissions per vehicle in the past 20 years. However, during that time the total miles travelled has doubled, resulting in higher levels of air pollutants in many parts of the UK.

Cars emit large amounts of carbon dioxide, which traps the earth's heat and causes global warming. Transport accounts for about one-quarter of the man-made greenhouse gas emissions from the UK. In addition to CO_2, motor vehicles generate three major pollutants: hydrocarbons, nitrogen oxides, and carbon monoxide.

Cars release pollutants from the exhaust as the result of the fuel combustion process, and from under the bonnet and throughout the fuel system when heat causes fuel evaporation. Evaporative emissions occur:

• When outside temperatures on hot, sunny days cause a car's fuel to evaporate;

• When the hot engine and the exhaust system of a running car cause the fuel to become heated;

• When the car is shut and remains hot enough to cause fuel to evaporate;

• During refuelling, when petrol vapours escape into the air from the petrol tank and the nozzle.

Cold Start

The greatest amount of exhaust pollutants are released during the "cold start" phase, or the first few minutes it takes a car to warm up. Since a car warms up faster when it is moving, drivers are advised to limit warm-up time. This is particularly relevant to the school journey, which is often less than three miles. For example two short journeys of three miles produce more CO_2 than a six mile portion of a longer 20-mile journey. Combining trips decreases motor vehicle emissions since it reduces the number of cold starts.

If we are to succeed in tackling climate change, the involvement of individuals is critical. We need to reduce the amount of damaging emissions that are released by the burning of fossil fuels. Cars are a source of considerable pollution at the global level, and account for a significant fraction of the total greenhouse gas emissions.

A passenger in a car can breathe in three times the amount of pollutants of a pedestrian or a cyclist, especially when, as often occurs during the school run, the car is idling in a traffic jam; each car in the line is sucking into its interior the pollution from the one in front, creating a tunnel of scum – not good for the adult driver and not great for your children.

My personal experience is that some children and parents are very interested in the science and most are aware of the negative impact of car travel, but, to see how their behaviour matters, they need concrete illustrations like:

• Driving an average journey to school (2.4km to primary school) produces enough CO2 to fill 70 UEFA footballs;

• Just one person who switches from driving to cycling to work (or school) during the week over a 7.5km trip each way saves about one tonne of greenhouse gas emissions a year.[48]

---

[48] Verity Firth New South Wales Minister for Environment and Climate Change

Appendix Three

The political context

The political context

Walking is one of the first things a child wants to do and one of the last things an adult wants to give up. It might seem that as a society we take walking for granted. And yet in the most recent Dept for Transport survey (of 22,000 people in the UK), 24% stated they had not taken a walk of 20 minutes or more in the past year!

It is instructive to see the way government transport policy has evolved over the last 30 years and not always in step with changes in public and/or expert opinion. Margaret Thatcher's famous comment: "A man who, beyond the age of 26, finds himself on a bus can count himself as a failure", set the tone for her administration, which regarded road-building as the *sine qua non* of economic prosperity and growth. Support for alternatives to the car was almost non-existent during this period.

In 1989, with the publication of National Road Traffic Forecasts, the government finally realised that this policy was counter-productive. Following a number of events in the 1990s (the BMA[49] report on cycle safety, the Earth summit in Rio de Janeiro in 1992 and the Royal Commission on Environmental Pollution's report on transport and the environment) the political climate started to change. It was finally acknowledged that new roads simply created more traffic and that this level of growth was unsustainable.[50]

Writing in 1993, John Adams[51] made the point that government transport policy consisted of promoting an explosive growth in the modern means of travel (cars and planes) and phasing out the 'old fashioned' means of movement (walking, cycling, buses and trains). In 1996, for the first time, support for cycling emerged with the National Cycling Strategy and with a White Paper *A New Deal for Transport: Better for Everyone*. The new deal was to make cycling and walking more attractive.

Hopes that the new Blair government in 1997 would adopt a radical approach were soon dashed. There was an appetite for change that John Prescott as Transport Minister could have taken advantage of but New Labour was afraid of upsetting the status quo. Admittedly 'two jags' did not set a good personal example either, and he probably came later to regret the remark , "I will have failed if in five years' time there are not many more people using public transport and far fewer journeys by car." In fact since 1997

---

[49] *British Medical Association*

[50] *In their seminal report (SACTRA, 1994) the UK Standing Advisory Committee on Trunk Road Assessment concluded that "induced traffic" was likely to occur as a result of road improvements.*

[51] *B Author of One False Move; a study of children's independent mobility*

road traffic levels have risen by more than 11% although train use has also risen and bus use has risen in London (where it is subsidised). Between 1997 and 2005, carbon dioxide emissions from road transport rose by almost three per cent, and currently account for more than one-fifth of total UK emissions. They were forecast to rise by a further 18% between 2005 and 2020, when they will represent in excess of 26% of total UK emissions. The cost of motoring has fallen in real terms by more than 8% under Labour, while the cost of public transport has risen: bus fares by 14% and rail fares by 5%. Although some MPs were keen advocates of the environmental transport agenda (Ben Bradshaw and Jeremy Corbyn for example) these issues were simply not high enough priorities for the government.

The reaction to the fuel escalator, which included haulage companies blockading the fuel depots in 2000, led many to portray the government as 'anti-motorist' and stimulated widespread protests. (Incidentally I found on a local level that it provided a well-needed boost to our campaign as many parents decided to save money by leaving their cars at home and discovered that the journey on foot was actually quite enjoyable!) But it did make the government even more wary of appearing anti-motorist. Meanwhile, the Conservatives had come up with recommendations for reducing the rate of traffic growth, which the government rejected in favour of increasing motoring costs substantially and hoping that this would have the same effect.

 FACT! *In the last 50 years car traffic has increased by 1,500%*

The National Walking Strategy was not given the massive launch it deserved lest it be seen as yet another 'anti-car' measure. Instead it was delayed and watered down and finally replaced by an advice document Encouraging Walking: Advice to Local Authorities. Defending the fact that of the thousands of staff employed by DETR,[52] only two people had responsibility for walking (which represents after all almost one-third of all journeys) Lord MacDonald, the Minister of State for Transport, could only remark "I suspect it is about right... .because most of us know how to do it... .I just think you can take a lot for granted when it comes to walking."

Progress since then has been mixed – ironically the London mayor who couldn't ride a bike was the man who did the most for cyclists and for environmental transport generally in London. Ken Livingstone's introduction of the congestion charge in London in 2003 showed that there were other effective ways of encouraging the shift away from motoring. Transport for London's monitoring exercise has shown that congestion in the zone fell by 30% while the volume of traffic within the zone went down by 15% meeting the targets set. More than five years after the congestion charge was launched, and over a year after the western extension was added, traffic in central London remains 21 per cent lower than pre-charge levels and traffic entering the extension has fallen by 14 per cent. There has been a 72 per cent increase in the number of cyclists on the capital's major roads since 2000.[53]

 FACT! *Roughly half of all London car trips are shorter than two miles, and another one-third are less than five miles.*

There is not yet enough evidence to assess the impact of the election in 2008 of Boris Johnson, a real cyclist, as Mayor of London. He is carrying out Ken Livingstone's commitment to copy Paris and install 6,000 hire bikes in London, his target is to get 5% of journeys on bikes, and comments like "a cyclised city is a civilized city" are music to the ears of environmental transport campaigners. On the other hand, Boris has allowed motor bikes in bus lanes, he has stood back from Ken's commitment to charge 4 4s, and he has agreed to get rid of the congestion charge in the western zone. The general public is, in theory, much more aware of the impact of car use on the environment, but the reality is that many find it hard to change their habits.

Nationally, the impact of the government's education policy on increasing parental choice and the introduction of 14-19 diplomas will have implications for sustainable travel policies.

The importance of investing in school transport solutions was clearly recognised in the March 2009 report from the House of Commons Transport Committee on School Travel. It concluded that: " There is no single 'magic bullet' solution to improving school travel…While there are benefits to reducing car use and encouraging walking and cycling where appropriate, no single mode is suitable for everyone to use. Government and local authorities should work with schools, parents and students to encourage them to consider the impact of different forms of transport. Safe and suitable alternatives to car use for children and young people must be provided, be they public transport, dedicated school buses, walking schemes or safe cycling." They also recommended that the government should make a clear commitment to promoting walking and cycling as the preferred transport options and that the amount of funding available to support walking and cycling should be increased.

[52] *Department of Transport, Environment and the Regions*

[53] *http://www.london.gov.uk/view_press_release.jsp?releaseid=10851*

Appendix Four

Best Practice Newsletter

Safe Routes to School

Walk to School Week 18th -22nd May

National Walk to School Week will be taking place in the week commencing 18th May. After last year's enormous success, we are now planning for this year.

Why Walk to School?

Walking to school is well worth it! Below are just some of the reasons:

S = SAFETY TRAINING

Walking regularly with a child from a young age enables them to develop life skills; preparing children with road safety and personal awareness skills.

C = CONGESTION reduction

Fewer cars on our roads is good for the environment and local communities; fewer cars at the school gate can make it safer for pupils making their way to and from school.

H = HEALTH benefits

Walking to and from school allows adults and children to incorporate physical activity into their daily routines.

O = ON the ball at school

Pupils who walk to school arrive wide awake and are therefore more prepared for the school day ahead.

O = OUR fun and friendship

Friends and family can walk to and from school together and enjoy some quality time.

L = LEARNING for life

Walking regularly enables a child to become more familiar with their surroundings and provides them with the opportunity to learn about the weather and changing seasons first hand.

WOW

Walk once a Week is a continuing success. Children have been collecting their WOW badges by walking, scooting or cycling to school once a week. The children who participate really enjoy receiving their badges once a month. It is not too late to join in if you have not already done so. Don't forget to ask your teacher to tick your name on the chart on the days you walk to school.

What is Walk to School Week?

The 18th-22nd May is National Walk to School Week. The Walk to School Campaign asks parents and teachers to think about their journey to and from school and the many benefits of making it on foot.

DUCKS will be participating in this initiative by encouraging pupils to consider how they travel to school and to think about how they could reduce car use by walking, cycling, using a scooter or public transport. This is not just for those who live close to school. It would be fantastic if families who have to come by car could park further from the school and walk the last five or ten minutes.

We hope to be able to use the Sports Centre car park again this year for those of you who may not be able to walk all the way to school. We would also like to organise the walking bus groups which were very popular last year.

To make this week a success we will need as many parent volunteers as possible. Please complete the attached form letting us know how you would like to help during the week.

Stickers will be given to children who participate in the scheme on each day. The class with the most stickers at the end of the week will win the much coveted Walk to School Week Cup.

DUCKS Parking

Please could we remind you of the parking restrictions at DUCKS.

- **Use the walkways and do not walk through the staff car park.**
- **Do not obstruct the lower car park walkway (leading from the gate off College Road to the Infants School) when parking.**
- **Drive as slowly as possible when entering and leaving the site.**
- **The staff car park is for staff use only at all times.**
- **The lower car park is for parents of children in the Kindergarten and Nursery classes and for parents who have a special need. If you require a Lower Car Park Pass, please see Ros or Polly. PLEASE DO NOT USE THE CAR PARK UNLESS YOU HAVE A PASS.**

The Lower Car Park time restrictions are as follows:

Before School: Driving in from 7.50am out by 8.20am

School Time: Driving in between 8.30am and 8.55am and out between 9.00am and 9.10am. (No cars may leave the parking area between 8.30am and 9.00am)

End of School: From 2.45pm cars can flow in and out. All cars must be out of the parking area by 4.45pm at the latest.

Thank you for your support and co-operation.

Appendix Five

Junior School assembly

Sample Junior School assembly

GOOD MORNING EVERYBODY.

My name is *[xxx]*. For those of you who don't know me I have a *[son in year x and a daughter in year x]*. We are all very keen on walking and biking to school so the headteacher has asked me to come and talk to you this morning about *[walk to school week/car free day]*. I want to talk to you today about how you get to school, WHY this is happening and what you can do either tomorrow, next week or any other day.

Let me ask all of you, if you don't have a car or if your mum or dad had to leave the car at home, what other way could they get to work, school or the shops?? (Walk, bike, bus, train)

Let me just ask the teachers who are a little bit older than all of you!…When you were at school… How many of you walked to school? *[say about…assess %]* How many cycled? *[assess]* How many took the bus? *[assess %]* How many by train? [assess %].

You see most walked to school partly because people were just used to walking more and fewer people had cars. You might be surprised to hear that a lot of children played in the streets even in big cities. I used to love playing football in the streets and we used to have a great game where four of us would bike in a row holding each others' hands (not the handlebars) because there was NO TRAFFIC – could you do that now? NO WAY

OK, now let's see how that compares with today's pupils…How many of you come to school by

Car, Bike, Bus, Train?

So compared to when your teachers at school *[at least twice]* as many go by car.

Let's not forget that **the car is a fantastic thing to have** – it is nice and cosy on a rainy day and we can sit inside listening to music or the latest Harry Potter book on tape and we can drive into the country for the weekend, it gives us untold freedom. Don't misunderstand me I am not anti-car, but some children have told me it is pretty boring sitting in the car while your mum or dad listens to the news on the radio and gets cross with all the rest of the traffic.

Can anyone tell me about some of the good things about other forms of transport – hands up someone who comes to school by bike….What's your name? What do you like about coming by bike?…………Hands up someone who walks in anything you like? What are other advantages of walking to school? *[keeping fit, feeling independent, chatting with your friends…]* Does anyone come by train or bus? What do you like?

Now what is good about going in the car? Can someone tell me..?

[Faster, go further, keep dry…]

Yes of course BUT there are also problems. If the number of cars on the roads in cities and in the country just keeps going up and up and up. **If all your children when asked in 20 or 30 years say that they all come by car…..Can anyone tell me what problems that could bring?**

[More pollution – which is not good for the planet is it?

More accidents – you are more likely to be in an accident in a car and you can endanger others,

More illness – does anyone have asthma here? Asthma has increased dramatically in polluted towns…people can also get overweight if they don't exercise regularly and that can lead to health problems can't it?

More noise]

The idea of the *[walk to school week/car-free day]* is to have a day or a week in the year rather like NO SMOKING DAY to try to get people to do without their car and find out what it's like, how the streets change, how people change!

So all over the country, schools will be encouraging their pupils to walk or bike to school even if it is only for the last 100 yards or so. In France a few years ago, they closed 40 miles of streets for a day to encourage people to abandon their cars and the people there liked it so much that they wanted to do this every week! What else did they say?

They said after the day that they had rediscovered their town as a more peaceful, tranquil place; they had met their neighbours for the first time. Noise levels had halved, which makes a big difference just to give you an idea of what that means – does anyone have any noisy loud pupils in their class??? Could you all point to the noisiest child in your class? OK, could I have ten of you standing up? You, you and you…

Now what kind of noises do cars make?

Hooting

Sirens

Screeching

All together, I want you to make your noise as loud as you can…..PRETTY AWFUL ISNT IT? That's the sound of traffic on a normal day outside the school.

BUT NOW LET'S stop and pause and be quiet and see if we can hear any birds outside…….. That's the sound of a *[day/week]* without cars and that's the sound we want to hear….

So I would encourage all of you to go home and tell your parents that you want to leave the car at home for a change and see what is like to walk or bike.

We want to make it a **SPECIAL DAY** for you if you walk or bike even a bit of the way. If you do, you will get one of these fantastic stickers to show how well you have done and you are also are allowed to *[wear your trainers/get a ticket to the cinema/win a prize for your class etc]*.

Before I go, here are just a few tips for you if you do usually come to school on foot, by car or are planning to come by bike.

For **WALKERS:** if you walk already it is always more fun to walk with your friends so ask your parents if they know other children who live nearby. Maybe they are nervous about walking in on their own. Maybe you could help them with the route.

For those in the CAR:

1. Firstly, talk to your parents about whether or not you could walk instead and get fitter. You could meet your mates on the way in and find out about your neighbourhood?

2. Second, if you live too far away why not think about sharing your car, taking a neighbour in your car or picking someone up on the way?

3. Third - why not talk with your mum or dad about driving some of the way and then walking the rest of the way to school? Your parents have had a form from school telling them where the meeting points are, so ask them and see if it could help your journey.

For the **BIKERS**:

1. Always wear a helmet – you can never be too careful.

2. You can cycle on the pavement if you are younger than [xx] but always watch out for people who are walking especially very young and old people.

3. Finally, don't forget that you MUST get off your bike when you enter the school grounds.

Thanks very much for listening everyone. Just remember when you go home after school to talk to your mum or dad about trying to walk or bike in. That way you'll be doing your bit for the environment and getting fit as well.

Appendix Six

Parental consent form

Parental consent form (Alleyn's Junior School: Safer Routes to School)

Dear parent,

Please find below details of the pilot 'walking bus' and 'Drive and Drop' schemes that will run every morning during walk to school week (insert relevant dates). We look forward to your participation in the scheme and hope it will be an enjoyable experience for your children.

Walking Bus routes:
1. Assembly point: xx; Assembly time: xx Departure time: xx, Route Co-ordinator: xx Contact no. xx
2. Assembly point: xx; Assembly time: xx Departure time: xx, Route Co-ordinator: xx Contact no. xx

Drive and Drop routes:
3. Assembly point: xx: Assembly time: xx Departure time: xx, Route Co-ordinator:xx, Contact no. xx
4. Assembly point: xx: Assembly time: xx Departure time: xx, Route Co-ordinator: xx Contact no. xx

• Each route has been risk assessed and volunteers trained.

• There will be a maximum ratio of 10 children-per-parent volunteer.

• Volunteers will wear high-visibility garments and stick to the set route.

• If there are two volunteers, one volunteer will walk at the front of the bus 'The Driver' and the other at the back of the bus – 'The Conductor'.

• Children will be expected to walk in pairs and not lag behind. They must follow the volunteers' instructions at all times.

• You are responsible for your own property. Carry your own bags.

Please ensure your child is aware of his/her responsibilities whilst participating in the walking bus. Children who misbehave will be reported to the co-ordinators and may be removed from the scheme.

All parents and children must sign the consent form below. If the number of pupils exceeds the capacity of the volunteers, your child may be refused a place on the walking bus.

Please fill in the enclosed slip and return it to your class teacher by (insert relevant date)

I agree to follow the code of conduct of the walking bus.

Your name _____

Child1:_____

Signature_____

Child2:_____

Signature_____

Route Number: _____

Emergency Contact No: _____

Which days? _____

• I give permission for the children named above to participate in the walk to school week scheme.

• I understand that they participate at their own risk.

• I have read the information and have told my child about the importance of good behaviour

Signed: _____

Date: _____

Appendix Seven

School Surveys

Best Practice - Sample Primary Parent Questionnaire

Alleyn's Junior School Safer Routes to School Questionnaire

As you are probably aware, we are attempting to raise awareness of safer routes to school and reduce car use. It is essential to develop this scheme and try out pilot schemes in the summer term to know how you currently get your children to school and if you are happy with these arrangements. We would be grateful if you could return this questionnaire, plus any comments you would like to make, to your child's class teacher by [insert date]. Many thanks for your time. All responses will be treated with the strictest confidence.

Q1. How far from Alleyn's Junior School do you live? (Please tick one box)

Less than one mile
One to three miles
Four to six miles
Over six miles

Q2. How does your child usually travel to/from school? (Please tick one box for 'to school' and one box for 'from school')

	to	from
on foot		
by bicycle		
by school bus		
by bus		
by train		
by car		
Combination of modes (please state)		

Q3. Who does your child normally travel with? (Please tick one box for 'to school' and one box for 'from school')

	to	from
A parent		
A parent & children /siblings who attend Alleyn's		
A parent & children/ siblings who attend other schools		
Other adult		
Other adult & children /siblings who attend Alleyn's		
Other adult & children /siblings who attend other schools		
On own		
Other children /siblings only who attend Alleyn's		
Other children /siblings only who attend other schools		
Other (Please State)		

171

Q4. Please indicate your three main concerns with the journey to/from school (1- most important, 2- next important, 3 - important)

Traffic congestion on the roads

Difficulty in parking

Traffic congestion around and in the school.

Inconsiderate road users
Danger for children
from road traffic.

Bullying by young people

Adult 'strangers'

Lack of safe cycle routes

Lack of provision for cyclists in school

Lack of exercise for children

Other (please state)

Q5. What would be your preferred mode of travel for your child to and from school?

Q6. What would be your child's preferred mode of travel to and from school?

Q7. Which of the following measures might affect your decision about how your child gets to and from schoo l?(Please ring as applicable. Once completed please go to the relevant questions for the suggestions for which you have marked Yes / Maybe. Then go to question 15.)

Improvements to the route (for walking)
Yes   No   Maybe   Go To Q8

Safer road crossings
Yes   No   Maybe   Go To Q9

Restriction of vehicle movement in school
Yes   No   Maybe

More road safety education for children
Yes   No   Maybe

Provision of a 'walking bus'*
Yes   No   Maybe   Go To Q10

Information on the safest routes
Yes   No   Maybe

More safe cycle routes to the school
Yes   No   Maybe   Go To Q11

Cycle training and cycle facilities in school
Yes   No   Maybe

Fewer items for children to carry
Yes   No   Maybe

Improved public buses
Yes   No   Maybe

Shuttle bus around local schools
Yes   No   Maybe

More school bus routes
Yes   No   Maybe

'Drive & drop points' from where children
would be accompanied on foot to school
Yes   No   Maybe   Go To Q12

Lift sharing scheme
Yes   No   Maybe   Go To Q13

Staggered arrival times at local schools
Yes   No   Maybe

Other (please state) / further comments
Yes   No   Maybe

Q8. Complete this question only if you
replied yes or maybe to question 7A

i) At which location would you like to see
improvements?

ii) What kind of improvements would
you like to see?

Q9. Complete this section only if you
replied yes or maybe to question 7B

i) On which road would you like crossing
to be made safer?

ii) What kind of crossing facility do you
feel would be appropriate?

Q10. Complete this section only if you
replied yes or maybe to question 7E

Along which route could your child join
a 'walking bus'? (Please tick one or more
boxes)

Half Moon Lane, East Dulwich Grove
Dulwich Village, Calton Avenue
Lordship Lane, Playfield Crescent
Other (please specify)

Q11.Complete this section only if you
replied yes or maybe to question 7G

i) At which location would you like to see
improvements?

ii) What kind of improvements would
you like to see?

Q12. Complete this section only if you
replied yes or maybe to question 7M
Where would be the most suitable place
for you to drop off your child for them to
walk accompanied to school? (Please tick
one or more boxes)

Sainsbury's, Dog Kennel Hill
Court Lane, Dulwich Park
College Road entrance, Dulwich Park
Turney Road, Dulwich Village
Top of Greendale, just off Denmark Hill
Other (please specify)

Q13. Complete this section only if you replied yes or maybe to question 7N

i) When would you be prepared to give another child a lift?
(Please tick one or more)

In the morning on the way to school

In the afternoon at 3.30pm

ii) When would you most appreciate a lift for your child?
(Please tick one or more)

In the morning on the way to school

In the afternoon at 3.30pm

iii) How many spare places to you have in your car? (Please fill in as appropriate)

On the way to school   places

In the afternoon at 3.30pm   places

Q14. Would you/your child be interested in either of these after school clubs?

Safe Routes to school
Cycle maintenance & safety

Thank you for taking the time to fill in this questionnaire
Please return to the school office

Q15. Some of these ideas need the help of good-hearted volunteers. Please could you indicate below if you would be willing to be part of a group of volunteers, even for as little as an hour a week.

Help to run the local lift-share database

Accompany a group of pupils 1 morning a week from one of the drop off/walking bus points detailed above (pls specify which)

Be part of a parent patrol outside the school

Assist with after-school club to promote pedestrian safety and/or cycling

Communicate with Southwark Council

Help with publicity and meetings

Q16. Do you have any other general comments or suggestions?

Name of child at Alleyn's Junior School
Class_____
Your name _____
Address _____
Contact telephone number _____

Finally, we would be grateful if you could indicate on the attached map the route your child takes to school. Please indicate whether they are walking, driving or cycling.

Primary Parents Self Completion Travel Survey

School Name _____

Date _____

1) Pupil's name: _____

2) What is your postcode?

1st Part _____   2nd Part _____

3) Do you take your children to school?
      Yes, every day
      Yes, sometimes
      No, never

4) How far do you travel to school?
      Less than 1 mile
      1 – 2 miles
      2 – 5 miles
      More than 5 miles

5) How long does it take you to travel to school?
      Less than 15 minutes
      15 – 30 minutes
      More than 30 minutes

6) How do you travel to & from School?

	To School	From School
Foot		
On foot with others		
Bike		
Bus		
Train / tube		
Taxi		
Car-share		
Car, not shared		

7) Do you change the way you travel to school depending on the weather?
      Yes
      No

Thank you very much for taking the time to fill in this questionnaire

8) How many cars are there at home?
      None
      One
      Two
      Three or More

9) Are you happy taking your children to school as you do now?
      Yes
      No

10) If you are not happy taking your children to school as you do now, how would you prefer to take them?
      Foot
      On foot with others
      Bike
      Bus
      Train / tube
      Taxi
      Car-share
      Car, not shared

11) Would you be interested in a "walking bus" scheme organised by parents within the school?
      Yes
      No

If yes, would you be willing to help walk the children to school?
      Yes
      No

Would you be happy to help organise a walking-bus?
      Yes
      No

12) Why do you choose your current method to take your child(ren) to school?

13) How could your child's journey to school be made safer for cycling or walking?

Secondary Parents Self Completion Travel Survey

School Name _____

Date _____

1) Pupil's name:_____

2) What is your postcode?

1st Part _____   2nd Part_____

3) Do you take your children to school?
    Yes, every day
    Yes, sometimes
    No, never

4) How far do you live from school?
    Less than 1 mile
    1 – 2 miles
    2 – 5 miles
    More than 5 miles

5) How long does it take your child to travel to school?
    Less than 15 minutes
    15 – 30 minutes
    More than 30 minutes

6) How does your child travel to & from School?

	To School	From School
Foot		
On foot with others		
Bike		
Bus		
Train / tube		
Taxi		
Car-share		
Car, not shared		

7) Does your child change the way they travel to school depending on the weather?
    Yes
    No

8) How many cars are there at home?
    None
    One
    Two
    Three or More

9) Are you happy with the way your child/ren travel(s) to school?
    Yes
    No

10) If you are not happy with the way your child/ren travel(s) to school, how would you prefer them to travel?
    Foot
    On foot with others
    Bike
    Bus
    Train / tube
    Taxi
    Car-share
    Car, not shared

11) Why have you and your child/ren chosen to travel to school the way you do?

12) How could your child/ren's journey to school be made safer for walking or cycling?

Thank you very much for taking the time to fill in this questionnaire.

School Staff Self Completion Staff Travel Survey

School Name_____

Date_____

1)Name _____

2)What is your home postcode?

1st Part _____2nd Part_____

3)Job Title:_____

4)How far do you travel to school?
    Less than 1 mile
    1 – 2 miles
    2 – 5 miles
    5 – 10 miles
    More than 10 miles

5)How long does it take you to travel to school?
    Less than 15 minutes
    15 – 30 minutes
    30 – 45 minutes
    45 – 60 minutes
    Over 60 minutes

6) How do you travel to & from School?

	To School	From School
Foot		
Bike		
Bus		
Train / tube		
Taxi		
Car (drive alone)		
Car-share		
Motorbike		

7) Do you own a bicycle?

    Yes
    No

8) Do you have a public transport season ticket?

    Yes
    No

9) How many cars are there at home?

    None
    One
    Two
    Three or More

10) What new modes of transport would you be willing to try?

    Walking
    Cycling
    Bus
    Train / tube
    Taxi
    Car sharing

11) How important is the provision of car parking on site to you?

    Very Important
    Quite important
    Neutral
    Not very important at all
    No Importance

12) Are there any improvements that you would like to see made that may encourage you to cycle, walk, use public transport or car-share with other staff?

i) Within the school site?

ii) Outside the school site?

13) Are there any issues of pupils' safety that you would like to raise?

14) Have you heard of the term "School Travel Plan"?

       Yes
       No

15) If yes, can you see the potential links between the development of a School Travel Plan and the curriculum?

       Yes
       No

16) Would you be interested in helping to develop the school travel plan?

       Yes
       No
       Maybe

Thank you very much for taking the time to fill in this questionnaire

Primary Pupil Travel Survey

School Name _____

Date_____

Class_____

Teacher name _____

No. of children in class on survey day

_____

No. of children absent on survey day

_____

Today we are doing a survey to find out about the way you normally travel to school (main mode by distance), and how you would prefer to travel to school. Please put your hands up in RESPONSE these questions. NB. it may be easier to ask younger children to move around, eg one corner of the classroom for those who walked, another corner for those who came by car, etc)

How do you normally get to school? (if 2+ modes used, just count main mode)

1. Who comes by car?
2. Who has a lift with someone else in a car?
3. Who walks to school?
4. Who comes on a bicycle or scooter?
5. Who comes by bus?
6. Who comes by train (or tube)?

TOTAL (1-6)
NB: MUST = total in class survey day.

How would you prefer to travel to school?

7. Car – own family?
8. Car lift?
9. Walk?
10. Bicycle or scooter?
11. Bus?
12. Train (or tube)?

TOTAL (7-12)
NB: MUST = total in class survey day

13. Do any of you stay on at school for clubs?

14. Do any of you go to an after-school club somewhere else?

15. Do any of you change the way you get to school depending on the weather?

16. Have any of you thought about getting to school a different way?

Please check that all the total boxes add up correctly to account for all children in the class on each question, and that you have filled in the information at the top of this form. Then hand it back to the STP co-ordinator in your school

Thank you very much for taking the time to fill in this questionnaire

Special School Travel Survey

School Name _____

Date_____

Class_____

Teacher name _____

No. of children in class on survey day

_____

No. of children absent on survey day

_____

Today we are doing a survey to find out about the way you normally travel to school (main mode by distance), and how you would prefer to travel to school. Please put your hands up in RESPONSE these questions. NB. it may be easier to ask younger children to move around, eg one corner of the classroom for those who walked, another corner for those who came by car, etc)

How do you normally get to school?
(if 2+ modes used, just count main mode)

1. Who comes by taxi?
2. Who comes by school bus?
3. Who comes by family car?
4. Who has a lift with someone else in a car?
5. Who walks to school?
6. Who comes on a bicycle or scooter?
7. Who comes by public bus?
8. Who comes by train (or tube)?

TOTAL (1-8)
NB: MUST = total in class survey day

How would you prefer to travel to school?

9. Taxi?
10. School bus?
11. Car – own family?
12. Car lift?
13. Walk?
14. Bicycle or scooter?
15. Bus?
16. Train (or tube)?

TOTAL (9-16)
NB: MUST = total in class survey day

17. Do any of you stay on at school for clubs?

18. Do any of you go to an after-school club somewhere else?

19. Do any of you change the way you get to school depending on the weather?

20. Have any of you thought about getting to school a different way?

Please check that all the total boxes add up correctly to account for all children in the class on each question, and that you have filled in the information at the top of this form. Then hand it back to the STP co-ordinator in your school

Thank you very much for taking the time to fill in this questionnaire

Covering Letter to Parents

On school letterhead

Date

Dear Parents and Carers

FUNDING TO HELP MAKE YOUR CHILD'S JOURNEY TO SCHOOL SAFER, HEALTHIER AND MORE FUN

We are asking everyone who travels to and from the school (teachers and other staff, parents, governors and children) to complete a short questionnaire asking about their journeys to school and transport choices.

Congestion and road safety issues around the school

You will be aware of the high levels of congestion around the school gate in the mornings and afternoons. We are looking to find ways to reduce the congestion, as well as make the children's trips to and from school safer, healthier, more sustainable and more fun! This work complements other work the school is already doing on road safety, health, the environment and citizenship – helping your children develop into healthy independent young people.

Funding

Funding is available to schools who carry out this kind of work looking at how their pupils and staff travel to and from school. This includes grant money, about £x thousand [insert relevant amount depending on type of school – speak to your STA] that can be used to purchase CCTV equipment, cycle parking, and wet weather waiting areas/shelters for parents, amongst other things. Additional funding will become available to improve safety on streets around the school.

How you can help (1)

Please fill out the attached survey – it is very important that we achieve a high response rate to this. It should only take you about ten minutes. (NB: If you have more than one child at the school and each brings a survey form home to be filled out, please only complete one form).

Many thanks for your time.

How you can help (2)

If you'd like to become more involved in helping to develop our School Travel Plan to increase walking and cycling to school, please do come and see me as soon as possible.

PLEASE RETURN THE QUESTONNAIRE FORM BY *[insert date here]*

Signed by

NB, if you would like any part of this letter or the questionnaire on audio tape or interpreted in your own language, please phone

Appendix Eight

School Travel Plans

School Travel Plan Template

(reproduced with kind permission of Southwark Council)

Description of the school:

Only needs to be one paragraph and if possible include an area map - (your Council School Travel Adviser should be able to help you with this)

- Location of the school site including pedestrian and vehicle entrances, surrounding roads, housing estates etc;

- Nearest public transport links (bus/tram stops, train/tube stations etc.);

- Number of car parking spaces on the school site - is this sufficient to meet staff and visitor demand? Are there any restrictions on who may use the spaces?

- Number of cycle parking spaces - is this sufficient to meet demand?

- Number of pupils and staff at the school;

- Description of the current catchment area of the school;

- Details of any out of school hours activities on the school site

Ethos of the School:

This paragraph indicates the other policies that your school has that link to the plan and explains why you are committed to developing and implementing a School Travel Plan

- Links to school vision (e.g. a commitment to the safety of pupils, promotion of independence, commitment to health and well being of staff and pupils, commitment to the environment etc);

- Links to healthy schools projects the school is engaged in;

- Links to Eco schools and Environmental education programmes the school is engaged in;

Baseline Information and Identification of Issues:

This information will come from your school surveys and anecdotal evidence where appropriate

- How do people currently travel to the school (staff and pupils)?

- Identification of problem areas e.g. particular road junctions, issues such as school gate parking, accidents rates, any other barriers to people using sustainable transport for the school journey.

- This could also include issues highlighted by OFSTED such as lateness or truancy, weakness in partnership working with parents, weaknesses in subject areas or key stages.

Evidence of Consultation and Involvement

- Parental surveys;

- Pupil surveys – not only existing mode of transport but also preferred mode;

- Discussions with the school council;

- Curriculum projects and class discussions;

- Assemblies;

- School Governors;

- Other stakeholders (e.g. community police officers, healthy schools coordinator, local residents, other schools etc).

What the school is doing already:

- Do you take part in Walk To School Week activities - if so what have you done in the past? (e.g. assemblies, stickers, curriculum work).

- If you have cycle storage how well is it used/promoted?

• Do your pupils receive cyclist or pedestrian training?

• Do you have a policy of using sustainable transport for school trips/journeys?

• Do you provide information to staff/new recruits/agency staff/visitors on how to get to your school by public transport?

• Does your prospectus discourage car use for the school run?

• Do you have a walking bus? If so how/where does it run? How many volunteers/children are involved?

• Curriculum - what do you currently do to teach road safety and /or environmental education? Do pupils have any lessons that have a transport theme?

This section should include anything your school is doing or has done that links to school travel and promoting sustainable, safe, transport.

Any items suggested here could form part of your action plan (referred to below) if your school is not currently involved in promoting/developing them.

Having established your "baseline" or current status, the next stage is to draw up an action plan.

The following pages provide some guidance on what you could include in your action plan - it is not intended to be an exhaustive or prescriptive list and you should identify actions that are relevant to your school.

Your Action Plan:

Basically setting out what you will aim to do to address the concerns and problems identified.

General points:

• Choose SMART targets (Specific, Measurable, Attainable, Realistic with a Timescale).

- Nominate a lead person or group for each target and/or step towards a target;

- Targets must have a timescale and an anticipated completion date;

- Lay the action plan out in a format that suits your school. A table is the most common format;

- Where funding will be required, indicate how much and where it might come from.

Set up a working group:

- Termly meetings to review progress and agree actions;

- Involve as many stakeholders as possible (e.g., senior management, governor, parent, council School Travel Adviser, School Council where appropriate, school police officer etc).

Walk to school campaign:

- Participation in the national and international weeks in May and October (your local council can provide materials);

- Walking on Wednesdays campaigns or other rewards scheme;

- Your action plan should detail what "participation" will mean for your school - will it include class activities, assemblies, sponsored walks, rewards/stickers etc.

Cycling

Your school may be reluctant to promote cycling for your pupils, particularly if they are of primary age, BUT, even in areas where there may be safety concerns related to the promotion of cycling to school, you can still provide or promote cyclist training for children (particularly those in Key Stages 2 and 3), parents and staff.

- Cyclist training - contact your local road safety officer;

- Cycle Storage - pupils will need a safe storage area for bikes when bringing them to school for training. Storage should be made available for staff and visitors;

• Cycle routes to and from your school you may be able to work with your council cycling officer to create routes;

• Participation in or promotion of Bike Week.

Walking Buses and/or other escorted walking schemes:

Your school may wish to set up a walking bus route(s) and assistance with this should be available from your School Travel Adviser or Road Safety officer. Steps to creation of the bus are:

• Investigation/feasibility of buses;

• Route selection and risk assessment;

• Recruitment of volunteers (including CRB checks);

• Training of volunteers and assemblies;

• Launch;

• Continued promotion with new parents.

A video showing the different ways that walking buses can operate to meet the varied needs of school communities with real case studies from London schools, is available from your School Travel Adviser.

Staff and Visitors:

• Provision of cycle parking;

• Provide information to staff on local authority staff season ticket loans, public transport links and timetables;

• Inclusion of maps and public transport link information provided to new and agency staff and visitors;

- Promotion of car sharing;

- A 1 in 5 campaign, where staff are encouraged to use sustainable transport for one day of the week;

- Ensure the travel plan is a regular agenda item at staff meetings;

- Encourage attendance at school travel plan training.

Curriculum:

Identify opportunities to link the messages and themes of your travel plan into the curriculum. This could be based in particular key stage or subject areas and/or could link to areas highlighted by OFSTED.

You will also need to identify any resources that will be needed to deliver a curriculum programme, including planning time.

Your LEA curriculum advisers and School Travel Adviser should be able to help in this area.

Marketing and Promotion:

- Regular items in the school newsletter;

- Information in the school prospectus and on the website;

- Availability of the travel plan to the whole school community;

- Dedicated notice board (or a section on an existing board) for updates;

- Provision of a case study report which could be used in London-wide best practice information.

Safer Routes Engineering Measures:

If your travel plan identifies problems that require an engineering solution, you will need to liaise with your local council engineering team - your School Travel Adviser will help with this.

Examples of engineering works could include:

- New signs and road markings;

- Traffic lights and controlled crossings such as pelicans;

- Zebra crossings;

- Speed tables or humps;

- Improved lighting;

- Pavement resurfacing;

- Cycle routes;

- One-way streets.

It is worth bearing in mind that engineering measures can be very expensive and your Council will have to bid for funding. This can mean that implementation may not be able to happen immediately.

Monitoring:

Your travel plan will have to show how you intend to monitor your progress and the process for reviewing the plan. For example:

- Inclusion in the school improvement plan;

- Annual surveys (these must be carried out);

- Termly hands-up surveys will provide seasonal data and indications of early successes;

- Annual report to governors;

- Evidence portfolio - this will provide a record of all the work you have done on the plan. It could include minutes from meetings, photographs of events and engineering measures, survey results, examples of pupil work etc. The portfolio will make it easy for you to update your plan and will allow your School Travel Adviser to quickly see the progress you have been making.

Sign Off and Formal Approval:

• The travel plan must be signed and approved by the headteacher and the chair of governors.

• You may wish to also have a representative from the PTA and the school council sign the plan;

• Following this the plan will have to be approved by your School Travel Adviser;

• Both council transportation and education departments will then sign it at assistant director level.

Best Practice

Alleyn's School Travel Plan

Alleyn's Independent School

2008
School Travel Plan

Part 1 – About the school

1.1 - Description

Alleyn's is an independent school for boys and girls aged 4 to 18. It was established as part of the charitable foundation of Alleyn's College of God's Gift, which comprises a number of mostly educational charities, including James Allen's Girls' School and Dulwich College. There are 950 pupils in the senior school and 230 in the junior school, with staff comprising of 120 teaching and 60 support (both full and part time). Out of school hours, the school makes its facilities available free of charge under a Community Use scheme run by a director of community use and two duty managers. At the time of writing, the scheme has approximately 20 groups providing diverse activities such as football training, woodworking and a maths club.

Opening hours during term time and holidays are 8am-5pm.

1.12 - Location of the School

The school is located in the East Dulwich area of the London Borough of Southwark in South East London. The school is made up of a junior and senior school on one site located between Townley Road and Hillsborough Road, which is off East Dulwich Grove. Location maps of the site and showing the surrounding area can be found overleaf on pages 2 and 3. The school is very close to James Allen's Girls' School which is on the opposite side of East Dulwich Grove. The Charter School, Dulwich Hamlet Junior School and Dulwich Village Infants' School are also within easy walking distance. The Dulwich area is mostly residential, with quiet streets and plenty of speed bumps. It can be reached by road through the South Circular, which is often very busy, but there are many zebra and 'green man' crossings to facilitate the journeys of those walking to school.

The main senior school entrance is on Townley Road. Entrance through the front is facilitated by a zebra crossing on Townley Road to ensure the safe crossing of all pupils and staff. Those who walk to school through Dulwich Village will benefit from the low speed limit (20mph on most residential roads) and zebra and 'green man' crossings. The lower school pupils (years 7 and 8) have their own entrance on Hillsborough Road, and their safety is ensured through the 'green man' crossing on East Dulwich Grove. Junior school pupils access the site via both the entrance on Townley Road, by walking through the senior school, or via a secure gate entrance on Hillsborough Road.

Gates at the Lordship Lane end of Townley Road are open at the beginning and end of the school day, but otherwise kept locked for security. The gate halfway along Townley Road is used for minibus access only.

1.2 - Description of the catchment area

Pupils come to Alleyn's from a wide catchment area covering much of London, the majority from southern boroughs, but many pupils come from some areas of Greater London and North London. The 'Foundation Coach' service run by Dulwich College Enterprises on behalf of the three Foundation Schools (Alleyn's, JAGS and Dulwich College) enables those in years 5 and 6 or of secondary school age who live further afield to consider Alleyn's as a practical option. There is, however, a good take up of places by those living locally. Entry is selective and by assessment at 11+, 13+ and 16+. Pupils come from a wide range of feeder schools.

1.3 – Transport links and site access

The school is very well serviced by a variety of transport links, the nearest National rail link being at North Dulwich station, ten minutes' walk away, which is on the line from London Bridge to Sutton and Wimbledon. On average, four trains an hour serve this station. Thameslink (from Bromley in the South and towards Bedford in the north) and Victoria/Orpington services are available at Herne Hill Station, which is a 20-minute walk away. Bus numbers 37, 12, 40, 176, 185, 197, 312, P4, P13 and P15 all stop within a reasonable walking distance.

1.31 - Parking and car use

There are 80 car parking spaces on site.

In past school inspections, it was noted that the staff car parking occupied a large portion of the main playground space, and following a major planning application to build a new performing arts centre on the site, it was agreed that cars should be prohibited from entering the central playground area and this is now in force. This has created a much-needed safe outside social and 'kick about' space for pupils.

This was utilised through the addition of a new car park with access from Hillsborough Road and an existing car park near the junior school off Hillsborough

Road was cleared and resurfaced, together providing a total of 47 parking spaces.

The front of the school also accommodates 11 cars, with additional spaces for grounds staff and minibuses through a third entrance halfway along Townley Road. All staff who previously parked on site have been accommodated through these new sites to prevent the exacerbating-street parking problems.

The school has a policy of not allowing members of staff appointed since June 2002 to park on site. This is stated at interview. Although this has some impact on surrounding roads, the 2008 survey data shows that more staff are finding alternative routes to the school (walking, public transport etc). This is also helped by the school's policy of providing rented accommodation within walking distance to attract good newly qualified teachers.

Finally, a motorbike and moped parking zone has been allocated in one of the car parks.

1.32 - Cycle routes and facilities

The school is on cycle routes LCN 23 and LCN 25. LCN cycle routes are designed to be safe enough to be used by a competent twelve-year-old. Children are advised only to cycle to school if they have a cycling proficiency certificate and are confident cycling on or near busy roads, as it is illegal to ride on the pavement.

At the time of writing, there were 45 cycle spaces on site. A significant number of these have been introduced since 2002. These are generally of the 'Sheffield Stand' type and are protected by CCTV cameras. Bicycles parked on site have been targeted by thieves in the past, which put pupils off, but due to increased site security since 2002 this has now stopped and pupils are returning to cycling. There is only limited sheltered cycle parking and increasing need for better cycling provisions on the school site.

1.4 - Ethos of the school

The vision and values of Alleyn's, as agreed by the school's governors, can be summarised as follows:

"The school aspires to provide co-educational excellence with a first class all round education to those of high intellectual promise and academic potential, regardless of background, race, creed or financial means."

"Both the junior and senior schools are independent schools with a common purpose and shared philosophy centred on a tolerant, inclusive and liberal education valuing all aspects of the full breadth of a wide academic and co-curricular programme, offered within a caring, friendly, happy community united by shared values and linked closely to parents, former pupils and the local community."

"The schools seek to be recognised within the local and extended community as a force for the public good, offering open access and excellence without exclusion for those most able to benefit from an academic education, around the focus of godliness and good learning based on a Christian tradition."

1.41 - Health, safety and well-being within the school

The desire for an 'all round education' and to be a 'force for the public good' embodies our promotion of the benefits of a healthy lifestyle for our pupils and staff. Throughout the past two years, the school has focused on good health and fitness for both its pupils and staff, with a special focus on food. This has been enabled through the eradication of chocolate, crisps and fizzy drinks from the school vending machines and providing instead fresh fruit, healthier snacks and water or juice drinks. The school lunch menu has also been improved and now aims to incorporate helping pupils to gain five portions of fruit and vegetables daily, while also aiming to be appetising and varied. This new focus on health and fitness can be linked to the following objectives related to journeys to school:

• Promoting the health benefits of journeys on foot or by bicycle;

• Promoting and enabling the positive environmental impact of reducing journeys by car;

• Improving the social and learning environment of the school and the local environment by managing traffic congestion and school parking in adjoining roads.

These objectives will begin to improve the 'eco-friendliness' of the school – and ideally reduce the carbon footprint of the pupils and staff through ongoing recycling of paper, cans and bottles throughout the school, combined with actions to reduce congestion and therefore emission levels within the Dulwich area.

Alleyn's has a strict school trip policy which includes a rigorous risk assessment undertaken by the supervising member of staff prior to the actual trip taking place. In order to ensure that these are satisfactory and cover all elements of the trip, they are inspected and approved by the headmaster.

In order to ensure that any changes in health and safety policy are fully implemented and understood by all members of staff concerned, the school receives annual visits from Dr. Bowker of Oxford Safety & Risk Management to administer advice and further information.

The safety of all Alleyn's pupils and staff is integral to the school and has been improved via a series of fences to stop pupils and staff from entering the school via the building site for the new performing arts centre. Security in and around the junior school is particularly stringent, with secure card-controlled entrances from the Senior school and on Hillsborough Road.

The school has always followed stringent policies set down by the Health and Safety at Work Act (relevant to non-employees, in this case the pupils) in order to provide a safe workplace and school for all those who attend. These regulations are enforced by support staff employed by the school, including security staff who are present throughout the day.

Part 2 - Key current initiatives

2.1 - Local authority aims and policies

Within the last five years, Southwark council has highlighted the importance of transport as a 'key to health and prosperity' and in accordance with the Mayor's Transport Strategy (2001) developed its own Local Implementation Plan (2006) to map out how it will continue to improve transport provision across the borough. The plan focused particularly on the utilisation of sustainable modes of travel, the improvement of public transport and improved safety throughout Southwark.

In relation to the immediate local area the LIP highlighted the following:

• The need to improve facilities for pedestrians and cyclists in both Dulwich Village and Lordship Lane, with aims to replace street furniture, relay paths and footways and generally improve the 'usability' of both of these commercial centres for these users;

- A supplementary document, the Road Safety Plan (RSP) highlighted North and East Dulwich as a 'priority zone' for a blanket 20mph speed limit throughout;

- The need to reduce child casualties as a result of motoring accidents through increased education and training – highlighting the role of the STP in improving transport provision throughout the borough;

- The need to reduce reliance on the private car for commuting and general use by improving local transport provision. This will be done through creating further pedestrianised areas, the extension of the East London line and the completion of the London Cycle Network by 2012 and 2010 respectively.

Following this policy concentration on education, sustainability and safety, Southwark council fully supports the implementation of STPs and has produced its own set of guidelines to assist schools in developing their own. Peter Coello is the school travel plan co-ordinator who has a key role in assisting schools to meet their travel plan initiatives and apply for funding. The Safer Routes to School group meets regularly at the School and has representation from a wide group of local people and Southwark Council. Local councillors are also kept informed of the group's work, take an active interest and are invited to meetings.

2.2 - How is Southwark Council addressing these issues?

Since 2006, Southwark council has initiated the following actions:

- Cut down on harmful emissions from buses by being the first London borough to switch its fleet to the use of alternative fuels in June 2005, when 70 fleet vehicles were converted to biodiesel;

- Allocation of £15,000 to improve safety at Lordship Lane junction with Barry Road;

- Extension of 20mph zones in East Dulwich, backed by £160,000 of funding;

- Proposed allocation of £55,000 for the extension of Cycle Link 177 through Dulwich Village (Court Lane to College Road) and College Road Cycle path, with more than £200,000 towards improvements along the existing length of the route;

• £30,000 for the creation of a new signal junction along Route 185 on Lordship Lane/East Dulwich Grove;

• Provision of free cycle training for both junior school pupils and adults within the borough, provided by Cycling Instructor Ltd.

2.3 - What has the school done so far?

• The school has moved to a situation of almost complete pedestrian/vehicle segregation. An existing green pedestrian walkway from the designated pedestrian entrance on Townley Road through the site has become superfluous as car parking within the central playground areas is now forbidden (as aforementioned);

• The zebra crossing on Townley Road provides direct safe access to the pedestrian gate;

• A new security lodge has been constructed by the pedestrian entrance to welcome and register visitors onto the site;

• Large flower planters have been placed throughout the schoolnto stop vehicles (including delivery vehicles) from entering the pedestrian area of the central playground and side approach;

• All cycle racks are protected by CCTV cameras;

• The school regularly participates in 'green travel' events during the year (particularly 'Walk to School Week' which has been very successful);

• Increased communication between parents and staff on green travel matters (including end of term newsletters and communications with new parents);

• Provision of separate bins for recyclable waste (paper, cans, bottles) throughout the school;

• Limiting of car parking on site to make it available only to members of teaching staff hired pre-2002;

• To help reduce car use by making the Foundation coach service free for all staff, providing they fulfil chaperone duties.

• Incorporating green travel ethos into school policy by including measures in the school's development plan

2.4 - Steps being taken by parents, staff & the local community

In order for the school's travel plan to be carried out successfully, it is important to have both support and encouragement from key groups such as parents, staff and the local community.

2.41 - Parents

Parents will have to make the majority of changes regarding mode of transport and travel patterns. They need to be willing to assist their children in walking, cycling or using public transport. If parents are reluctant to allow their child to travel to school alone, car-sharing schemes or a 'buddy' partner system can be established with other parents and pupils in their local area. This is particularly significant for junior school children who are more vulnerable.

Walk to School week (2007 and 2008) was encouraged at Alleyn's, with a free ice-cream or drink offered to those who took part and walked every day. Although the school should aim to achieve high numbers of those who take part through increased promotion, it is important to realise that many older pupils (particularly within the upper school) will not be easily persuaded to participate. Therefore, a wider variety of incentives (if necessary) may help to achieve better results. Within the junior school there is considerable scope to turn such events into fun activities for pupils through walking buses and extra travel activities.

2.42 - Staff

The majority of the staff have not been actively involved with the project at Alleyn's, but following the proposed actions of cycling proficiency training and travel-themed assemblies in tutor periods, combined with further promotion of events such as 'Walk to School Week', staff will be required to provide more support and encouragement for pupils who choose to change their mode of transport. They will have to set a good example to the children of the school, showing that they are willing to change their mode of transport so the high level of car dependency is reduced.

Over the past two years (2006-8), Anna Blythe of the geography department has created an Environmental Society, which has pushed for (and implemented)

increased paper recycling throughout the school, and recently introduced the recycling of drinks cans and plastic drinks cups.

Part 3 – Travel patterns

3.1 – Survey results

Travel surveys were conducted in 2005 and 2008, making it possible to see a trend and display the positive impact of our work to date, particularly with pupils. The most recent 2008 survey was sent out directly to all parents (800 surveys), with the school's freepost address included to encourage parents to fill them in. The school achieved a 91% response rate.

The 2008 survey shows that 18% of children come to school by car (including 5% car sharing). A further 24% walk, 19% use the Foundation Coach Service, and 21% come by public bus. Of the remainder, 6% come by train and 6% by bike. The table below shows the contrast between these figures and survey results from previous years. The progress within the last three years is remarkably encouraging, with those taking public transport to school rising from 17% to 27% throughout the school, and those coming in by car reduced from 25% to 18%. The utilisation of public transport provision over the private car displays the encouraging effect of free bus travel for under 16s and reduction of parking space available around the school site.

2008 Results:

Mode	No. of Pupils	Mode	No. of Pupils
Family Car	191	Public Bus	223
Car (Self Drive)	11	School Bus	202
Car (Lift)	53	Train	64
Walk	254	Taxi	0
Bicycle	64	Motorbike / Moped	0

Mode of transport to school	Children (%)			Staff (%)		
	2002	2005	2008	2002	2005	2008
Family Car	37	25	18	0	0	N/A
Car (Self Drive)	0	0	1	62	57	38
Car (Lift)	6	4	5	3	3	8
Walk	21	25	24	18	23	33
Bicycle	1	4	6	2	2	7
Public Bus	6	12	21	7	5	9
School Bus / Foundation Coach	24	25	19	0	0	0
Train	5	5	6	7	7	7
Taxi	0	0	0	0	0	0
Motorbike / Moped	0	0	0	1	2	0
Total (%)	**100**	**100**	**100**	**100**	**100**	**100**

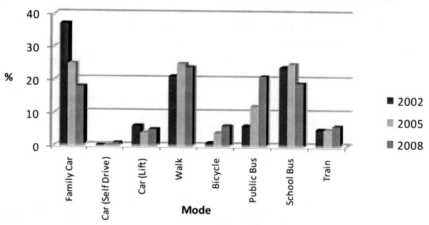

Graph showing modal shift in students actual travel mode

The 2008 staff survey was sent out in April to all staff in both the senior and junior schools, and over a period of six weeks 402 replies from the Senior School and 113 from the junior school were returned, again providing a sufficient sample area. Since 2005, the figures for staff travel are very encouraging, with 21% fewer staff travelling in by car since 2005. This can be attributed to the reduction of parking spaces on-site, and the policy of allocating spaces only to those employed before June 2002. The percentage of staff walking to the school has increased by 10%, with public transport use also increasing, although at a slower pace (up to 2%). Many staff highlighted issues of cycle facilities at the school, and the unreliability of public transport services. However, progress over the past five years has been steady and should be continued with further transport provision.

Part 4 – Consultation and involvement

4.1 – Integration of SMT and local council

July-August 2008

• Series of meetings with the bursar and senior admin staff to begin updating and expanding the travel plan;

• Much contact with TfL and Oyster to arrange the delivery of under 18s free travel pass forms;

• Contact with Peter Coello at Southwark council to discuss cycle training and with Roger Stocker (cycling officer) to obtain cycle maps for the school and its surrounding area, and to gain further information on cycling proficiency.

January 2008

• Bursar presented preliminary travel plan to the senior management team. It was greeted with enthusiasm and approval from all parties;

• Approval was granted to send out travel pattern surveys to all parents in the next general mailout.

February-March 2008

• Included in the survey was a letter explaining the school's 'green' initiatives, and in response many parents provided email addresses for further updates on travel information and eco-friendly tips from the school;

• Also included was the chance for parents/pupils to express any concerns or comments on the travel services to and from the school. Issues of safety on public transport were emphasised, along with concerns about cycling facilities.

4.2 – Partners in the school travel plan

The following committed and established group ensures the long term effectiveness of the travel plan.

Bursar at Alleyn's School
Alleyn's Governor
Parent (Alleyn's)
Bursar at JAGS
JAGS Governor
Parent (JAGS)
Dulwich Society
Southwark Council (Travel Plan Co-ordinator)
Southwark Council (Highways group)
Southwark Council (Cycling officer)
Foundation Coach Service
Local Ward Councillors
Local Police
Local Residents Associations
Bursar & Business Manager, Charter School
Governor, Dulwich Hamlet

4.21 - Safe Routes to School Group

Another key element in the implementation and development of the travel plan is the Safe Routes to School Group, for whom there has been growing support and interest among the parent body and community alike.

The group consists of representatives from the Dulwich Society, Southwark Cyclists, JAGS, Charter School, Alleyn's and the Dulwich Community Council. They meet on average four times a year to discuss issues of congestion, safer cycle routes, appropriate allocation of TfL funds and improving conditions for pedestrians throughout the Dulwich area. The group has successfully integrated the local community with parents and pupils of the School in the tackling of issues in the area.

Local councillors and police officers have now been brought into this framework, and liaison arrangements made with local residents' associations and societies.

Part 4 – Objectives of the school travel plan

4.1 – Aims for the school

The policy aims as set out previously by TfL have helped formulate the school's objectives for the travel plan;

- To encourage walking and cycling;

- To provide better facilities for those who do not drive to school (excluding those who car share);

- To address problems associated with car parking and congestion;

- Present sustainable transport modes as a viable alternative to the family car through the advertisement and encouragement of the use of local public transport links.

4.11 - What are the benefits of the STP?

- Healthier pupils and staff;

- Cleaner environment with fewer emissions and less congestion;

- Increased safety for vulnerable road users, including improved disabled access for 2008.

4.12 - Who will benefit from the STP?

- Staff;

- Pupils;

- The local community;

- Parents;

4.2 - Targets for the school

As the recent survey results show, use of the family car to travel to school has dropped by 7% since 2005, which is quite a significant change. Following this, it would be even more encouraging to see percentages of walkers and cyclists rise by the same amount by 2010. The targets, therefore, for Alleyn's are set out as follows;

Travel Plan Update	2005 survey results (%)	2008 survey results (%)	2010 survey results (%)
Walk/cycle	29	30	38

Part 5 - Actions required to achieve the objectives

The following table shows the current objectives and the actions needed to achieve those objectives

Objective 1: Encourage walking and cycling						
Action	Responsibility	Timescale	Target	Monitoring	Review by	Review date – completion date
Cycling proficiency training onsite and bicycle maintenance		2008 onwards	Raise numbers of qualified cyclists aged 11+, in turn providing them with the confidence to cycle to school	Annual pupil 'hands-up' survey, actual numbers of those who gain cycling proficiency	January 2009	N/A
Road safety education from local police, and lower school personal health & safety assemblies twice annually	Lower School Head & Deputy Head	September 2008 onwards	To ensure all pupils have road safety education at both key stages whilst at the school	Head of Lower School	July, annually	
Continue participation in 'Walk to School Week'	Masters & form tutors	Ongoing	Annual participation in WTS week		July, annually	N/A
Participate in 'Bike Week'	House Masters & form tutors	June 2008, annually	Annual participation in Bike Week		July, annually	N/A
Include TfL cycle route maps in every Welcome Pack for parents of new pupils		September 2008	Increase numbers of those cycling to school. Provide ample information on safe cycle routes		As and when TfL updates cycle routes and issues new maps	TfL will dictate
More cycle racks	Bursar, As funds allow,	2008 onwards	Evidence from surveys that cycle parking is not a problem	Bursar	Annually through pupil surveys	2008/9

Objective 2: To provide better facilities for those who do not drive to school (excluding those who car share)

Action	Responsibility	Timescale	Target	Monitoring	Review by	Review date – completion date
Provide information and application opportunities for Oyster Photocards, including those aged 16 and over.	School office	September 2007 onwards	Increase numbers of pupils travelling to school by bus		July, annually, through TfL website	As and when the Oystercard system is subject to change
Extension of bus route 42	Safe Routes group	Proposed by TfL in 2006, ongoing	Extension of route			Whenever TfL propose extension

Objective 3: To address problems associated with car parking and congestion

Action	Responsibility	Timescale	Target	Monitoring	Review by	Review date – completion date
Monitor parking to ensure only authorised vehicles are on site	Security guards	Ongoing	Only registered vehicles or those with permit parked onsite	Bursar		N/A
Promote car sharing through a database that parents canaccess and view other sharers in their area	Bursar	2008 onwards	Increase in car sharing and therefore less congestion and cars carrying only 1 passenger	Bursar	Continued	N/A

Objective 4: Present sustainable transport modes as a viable alternative to the family car through the advertisement and encouragement of the use of local public transport links

Action	Responsibility	Timescale	Target	Monitoring	Review by	Review date – completion date
Include a local public transport information pack in the Welcome Pack for parents of new pupils to the school	Admissions secretary	September 2007 onwards	Increase in public transport use amongst new pupils, and therefore throughout their school career	Through annual 'hands-up' pupil survey on travel mode	August 2008	N/A

Part 6 – Monitoring progress

Monitoring of the actions proposed under the travel plan will be undertaken by annual staff and pupil surveys, the results of which will be recorded and analysed, including a comparison to national average figures.

Monitoring the travel patterns of staff and pupils will include;

- Staff survey;

- Pupil survey of existing travel patterns and obstacles to improvement;

- Foundation Coach Data;

- Cycle parking census;

- Assessment of events and measurements of any long term change (ie. as results of events such as "Walk to School Week")

How changes will be reported

Immediate and urgent issues should be reported to the Bursar.

Date for review

Although the document will be updated with new survey data as it is available, the next major review of the travel plan will take place in July 2009.

Alleyn's School

Sign Off and Formal Approval

Our School Travel Plan has been approved by the chairman of our Safe Routes group on behalf of the Group, by the school's bursar (on behalf of the school's senior management team) and our Safe Routes Governor (on behalf of the school's Governors)

Signed …………………………………………..(group chairman)

Signed ………………………………………….. (bursar)

Signed ………………………………………….. (governor)

Our School Travel Plan has been approved by our school travel plan clerk

Signed ………………………………………….. (School Travel Plan clerk)

Index

Index

Further reading

A new deal for Transport?
Edited by Iain Docherty and Jon Shaw
ISBN: 978-1405106313

Car Sick: Solutions for Our Car-addicted Culture
by Lynn Sloman
ISBN: 978-1903998762

Children, transport and the quality of life
by Mayer Hillman
ISBN: 978-0853745723

The Walking Bus Guide - How to set up and run a walking bus
by T Allatt and S Marshall
ISBN: 978-0954916503

Cutting your car use
by Randall Howard Ghent and Anna Semlyen
ISBN: 978-0865715585

The Author

Ann Kenrick OBE, a keen cyclist and walker, has been involved in sustainable transport issues for over fifteen years as a Trustee of the Environmental Transport Association and of the London Cycling Campaign. She was also Founder and Chairman of the Safe Routes to School Group in East Dulwich, London. She has been recognised for this work with a Southwark Civic Award. She is also Secretary-General of the Franco-British Council.

The Illustrator

Henry Paker's first book, *Don't Arm Wrestle A Pirate*, created with comedian Dave Skinner, was featured on the Richard and Judy Book Club in Christmas 2007. In 2009 they will be publishing another cartoon book, *Why Steve Was Late*. He is also a stand up comedian who performs at the Edinburgh Festival and throughout the UK. In 2008 he won the Leicester Mercury Comedian of the Year title and came second in the Laughing Horse new act competition.

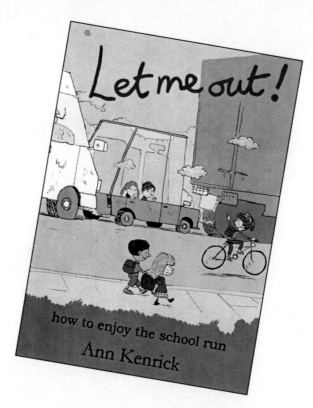

FREE DOWNLOADS

USE BOOK PROMOTION CODE *LMO0709*
TO DOWNLOAD THE FORMS AND QUESTIONNAIRES
IN THIS BOOK, AS WELL AS OTHER INFORMATION
AND IDEAS, FROM
THE LET ME OUT! WEB SITE AT

WWW.LOLLYPOPPUBLISHING.CO.UK/LETMEOUT

To order further copies of
Let Me Out! How to enjoy the school run
and for more information on the books published by Lollypop
please go online to
www.lollypoppublishing.co.uk
or contact customer services at
info@lollypoppublishing.co.uk

Lightning Source UK Ltd.
Milton Keynes UK
29 October 2010

162069UK00002B/1/P